HALFWAY THROUGH THE TUNNEL

HALFWAY

THROUGH THE TUNNEL

BARRY R. BERKEY, M.D.

PHILOSOPHICAL LIBRARY
New York

FIRST EDITION

Library of Congress Catalog Card No. 72-82790
SBN 8022-2099-1

Manufactured in the United States of America

TO VELMA

PROLOGUE

Books "about" psychotherapy are a dime a dozen. Stories "about" psychiatry, psychoanalysis, individual emotional problems and the effort to grow and change are filling libraries. This is not a book about psychotherapy. Do you ever wonder how the psychoanalyst keeps from getting bored to death? Do you ever wonder what goes on in his head as he listens? Do you wonder what he says in answer to those 10,000 questions that the patient keeps asking? The friend who wrote this book doesn't say a single word. Maybe we can get him to write another book. Even a good Jewish mother loses her temper when the kids go too far.

The story that is told here is not "about" anything. It's a word-of-mouth picture, cast upon a screen, showing how a woman, with her fifth psychotherapist, fights halfway through the tunnel to love, life, light and to the freedom to choose. Pam's camera is a beauty. Now it's wide angle gives you huge, panoramic pictures; even a kaleidoscopic sweep of all the things that have happened to her, and that pound their way through her head, hour after horrible hour. And then suddenly, she zooms in with her high powered lens for a close-up of her first analyst or her second analyst, her second boyfriend, her mother, the hell of washing dishes and changing diapers. Or sometimes it's a mug shot. Really, she does a lot of comparing between what goes on in her head and what goes on in her gut. If the therapist had said anything, it would have spoiled her pictures, as we'd just get the story. This is like one end of a telephone conversation. You're free to enjoy your own ideas of what's on the other end, but she gives you enough to feel a clear sense of the struggle, the pain, and the joy of trying to change. She's warm, she's anxious, she's bitter, she's authentic. It is as though, after four trials at psychotherapy, her concept of herself is still that of a nobody, and yet the reader hears the pain of her love for her child and her hatred, its glory and its horror. To those who have been on the couch, she talks in a fun, open, deliberate, honest way. To someone who has never been in psychotherapy, she's like the kid who's in swimming, saying to the boy on the bank, "Come ahead and jump. I won't let you drown."

Probably the force that makes this kind of psychoanalytic format especially intriguing to this reviewer, who is a family therapist, is the fact that it's done in collaboration with group therapy. She not only talks about herself and her life, she portrays the relationship between individual psychotherapy and group psychotherapy. The power of this open-ended group, the way she sees herself in the other people who make up the group, the way she shifts in her choices and in her freedom to love and hate—it's as if the individual therapy and the group therapy activate each other, as two drugs sometimes produce triple the effect.

Pam and her story have tremendous implications for professional training in psychotherapy, for those people who want to get up the courage to change themselves, for those people who are trying to figure out the relationship between group therapy and individual therapy. One even hears bits and pieces of why the previous four psychotherapies were not enough. Does this fifth one work? We don't really know, although the existential shift and the effort to get the spouse into therapy with her certainly denotes things are different. And maybe if you get halfway through the tunnel, it isn't so hard to get the rest of the way.

There are some interesting fringe benefits to this story. The most obvious one is that it is fun reading; less apparent is the fact that there's a great deal of human wisdom. Pam does have some professional training, so she is more of a subjective thinker than many patients, and she adds bits and pieces from that wisdom. In this, her fifth therapeutic trip, she knows how to be more honest, more raw, to share her despair and her euphoria with openness, and to let you see her chaos, and let you see, also, her love of her husband and her child. Furthermore, she's not preoccupied with transference as the end of living, but shows you the outside world as well. One of the other fringe benefits is Pam's way of describing people who are making it. It's as though she senses when human adaptation is successful, and doesn't just see her own story as all there is to life. She also gives us an entree to one person's struggle with death, and we see Pam's response to the loss of a loved one. These all come in the same kind of free, open way that helps the psychiatrist to know more about life, even if it's still just as hard for him to grow, as it is for you and me. Pam also knows how to hit you behind the head when she says, absence is more real than presence, and emptiness is more real than fullness. She adds a dimension to one's own perception of himself that makes life a little more livable, and makes the light at the other end of the tunnel a little more visible. It isn't often that you hear group therapy defined better: "Nine women sitting in deafening loud silence." Nor does one often hear the adolescent pain more poignantly said than, "I must have thought I was some sort of saint that I couldn't get pregnant." Any couple will respond when they read, "I hear my husband say, Pam, why are we killing each other. We love each other so fucking much. God, why do we do this to each other?" Just to listen to all the ins and outs of Pam's thinking is a very growthful experience; to have all these fringe benefits of wisdom and perspective on the person, the marriage, the experience of motherhood, and the experience of group therapy makes this book an exciting way of plunging into one's self-doubt and one's need for change. In fact, I'm left with a real question, "Does anyone ever get farther than halfway through the tunnel?"

CARL A. WHITAKER, M.D.
Professor of Psychiatry & Family Therapy
University of Wisconsin, Department of Psychiatry
Madison, Wisconsin

CONTENTS

PREFACE

One purpose in the making of this book is to acquaint the general reader with the true nature of the meaning of psychiatric care and what goes on behind the mysterious, closed door of the psychiatric office. Another object is to popularize the method of study of one's self, for gaining personal growth, inner knowledge, feeling and freedom. To lay to rest, or at least relax the myth that only deranged people seek and can benefit from psychiatric care is another implied message. All sensitive individuals interested in the mind, this most protean of subjects, will find the evolution that occurs in this collection of psychiatric sessions to be . . .

illuminating but confounding,
refreshing but exhausting,
appealing but repelling,
humorous but melancholy,
honest but profane,
touching but angering,
disjointed but with a thread of continuity.

People who are overly concerned with morality, who find profanity offensive, who in their approach to life find ways to avoid looking and seeing that which is not virtuous and noble may throw this book down in exasperation. People who dismiss as sinners those who do not conform to what they feel is right, and who insist on simple, superficial and tidy control of a tiny, selected and constricted segment of their world may feel frustration. For such individuals this book is not written. Simply stated, certain labyrinths of the mind cannot be explained in a monosyllabic, plain way.

The idea of organizing or neatly and creatively synthesizing the processes that go on in this book has never been seriously considered in order to avoid impairing realism. Communication and the soil of self-discovery contained and revealed within have been left almost as they were found—untouched, raw and real.

Carrying the burden of transmitting these messages rests upon Pam. She reaches into her past to tell you bluntly about her private world. She makes no virtue of the charms or defects in her present life, as she talks about Jeff, her husband, or Gilly, her son. Her feelings for her immediate family, parents and relatives, and for many significant others in her life would allow nearly every literate adult, male and female, to vicariously share and identify with the torment, pleasure and humor of her encounters. The ladies in Pam's Group Therapy group, from whom symbolic stimuli arise, contribute to the revealing repertoire of nude dialogue just as it rolled off the couch.

A year of visits, once-a-week in group therapy and once-a-week in individual therapy, constitutes the setting for this expressive, experiential delivery. Pam was deliberately chosen to carry the intended messages because of her provocative life style, her natural capacity for enthusiasm, her vigor and an approach to life that is real beyond usual conventions. Her defects are not applauded, but they are accepted and set forth at length, so as to communicate the endless variations of self-search.

To preserve total anonymity, all places are changed, some names are changed, other names are interchanged. It is possible that certain patients may not even recognize themselves. Further, many personal beliefs hitch a ride on the train as it winds through the tunnel. Where the events veer from fact, and the untouched is "touched up," it is because of these beliefs and the masks which adorn the tunnel dwellers. For these reasons, the boundary between fiction and nonfiction becomes blurry; purists would call this book a novel.

B.R.B.

ACKNOWLEDGEMENTS

One of the great benefits of writing this book, besides achieving the primary goal itself, is a valuable and unexpected by-product, the by-product of experiencing a totally new microcosm of humanity. Many people, responsible and caring people, came forth to provide help and encouragement. Their involvement is a rare and rewarding experience.

I wish to express my deep appreciation to a good friend and colleague, Dr. S. Norman Feingold, for his continuous encouragement and advice over many months, night and day, weekend and weekday. He generously created time from a busy schedule that allowed no time, to provide me with solid guidance, based on his having authored twenty-five books.

Very special gratitude is felt for Dr. Carl A. Whitaker, who endorsed this book by the honor of his writing the Prologue. Dr. Whitaker's influence upon me was great, both in shaping my career thinking, and in my approach to patients, and I am fortunate to have had such a man as a teacher—and now as a friend.

Dorsey Woodson, my main reader and technical advisor, and Eileen Gilmore, were of immense help early on, in converting chaos to order. Through the expertise and devoted effort by A. Susan David, I was unable to sneak poor grammar or too many misspelled words into this book. Dr. J. Pastoor, a man whom I have never even met, offered his time and ability to correct structural errors. Sandra

Crane, my loyal, patient chief secretary, typed the manuscripts through their progression and shared her enthusiasm and optimism, despite the sometimes tedious nature of her role. She was assisted by Ann Levin and Sue Walker, both of whom I wish to thank.

Pam and the ladies in the group: Margaret, Grace, Helen, Irene, Maxine, Jackie, Noreen, and Linda are real people with fictitious names. Except for Pam, who knew of this book, the others provided valuable, meaningful messages without their full knowledge, which are now passed on, so that we may all grow from their experiences.

My understanding wife was my greatest single source of help. From providing the title to this book, to many other suggestions and criticisms, to proof reading and correcting errors of all kinds, she was there with limitless, unselfish cooperation. How do I say thanks for her staying awake with me, helping while I wrote, for months of nights? Here is a labor of love, as well, for which there is no thanks.

To our children, Kent, Richard and Lori—thank you for being quiet. That's no small gift from three small kids.

The defects in this book—in word, deed or thought are entirely mine.

CHARACTERS

These people constitute the many strands that connect a segment of one life; a venture into darkness and confusion.

The Family

PAM (PAMMIE), who just is.

JEFF (JEFFY), Pam's husband who feels he gives but never gets.

GIL (GILLY), their son.

CINDY, Pam's niece who came to visit.

SARA, Pam's fecal sister, with whom she is angry.

IZZY (POP-POP), Pam's father who isn't a typical Jewish merchant.

MOM-MOM, the matriarch.

ROUTE 95, a highway with a vendetta for Jeff.

ROSALIE, Cindy's sister who cries.

THE COUCH, a place Pam feels she never leaves.

The Group

A mingling of fortunate strangers. Some come and stay. Others depart, but not before leaving their mark upon Pam.

MARGARET, the wall.

GRACE, the real one.

HELEN, claims to have been "there."

IRENE, ties ribbons on unsuspecting objects.

MAXINE, blah and boozing.

JACKIE, the fatty.

NOREEN, the best emotionally integrated stranger.

LINDA, the one who talks toast and tea.

xix

People from the Past

From Boston

CHUCK, in whom Pam had sexual interests.
LANA, his wife.
ALEXANDER, their child.

TIM, Chuck's friend in whom Pam had no sexual interest.
LILLIAN, his wife.

TOM HUNTER, a neighbor.
LORI, his girl friend.

DR. AUDREY SIMON, who confirmed Pam's suspicions about Myrna's illness.

From New York

PROF. DIETERDOFF, who gave birth to the concept of the "flip," a word to signify that the sun can shine through rain and clouds.

MURIEL, Jeff's foster mother.
HUGH, Jeff's foster brother.

MYRNA, the most influential, divine goddess in Pam's past.

JAN, sexy and with a great body, except for saggy boobs.
ROBERT, who had enough money to become her husband.
MONICA, their no-neck monster.
KRISTEN, their other child.

DR. APTITUDE, who fixed Gilly's eyes.

MIRIUM COHEN,
RUBIN COHEN,   with whom Pam lived in college.

DICK HORTON,
CLARA HORTON,   who begat the first Hercules.

CONNIE, who—to psychiatrist after psychiatrist—
        dumped the fact that her brother fucked her.
STEVE, her husband, the junky.

JUDY, the witch, the bitch, the yogi, and Myrna's closest
        friend.
ROGER, a writer of little success.
MYRNA, their daughter, named after big Myrna.

VIRGIN MARY, a leading figure in a best seller.
SCOTT, whose rats ate pellets rolled by Pam.
IVANOFF, the gymnastic masturbator.

ALLEN WILSON,
MARK,   two pals of Jeff's.

RITA, who dated Jeff; married Scott then killed herself.

HERBERT GROSS,   with whom Pam lived while in col-
MARLA GROSS,   lege, before living with Rubin and
                 Mirium Cohen.

CLOVIS DIAMOND, a Jungian analyst and close friend
    of Myrna's.
MAGNA MATERS, a group made up of many, i.e. Clovis,
    Myrna, other Jungians.
NICHOLAS, Myrna's lover for many years.

People from the Present

Washington, D. C.

NANCY, a neighbor.
PAUL, her husband.

LARRY,
BOB,   and dozens more who work in Jeff's section.

MOOG, a dragon with visual problems.
BUBBLES, his girl friend.

SPOOKY, who used to limp.

VON HOFFMAN,
ART BUCHWALD,   who aren't worth reading.

BARBARA HOWAR,
JUDITH MARTIN,   who are.

HERCULES II, who shits a lot.

SARA, a baby sitter whose brother balled her.
WILLY, her brother, who also baby-sits, whom Pam finds
     sexually arousing.

VIRGIL, the adult boy.
RICHARD NIXON, a politician who lives in a house with
     pillars.

The Doctors

Those who tried to help; who witnessed the poignancy
of Pam's being; who tried and tried and tried. . . .

GLADSTUN, from New York, who treated Jeff and was
     doctor number three for Pam.
ROSENBERG, number four from Boston.
KAPLIN, number one, when Pam was a college student.
OLSON, number two, who treated Pam after graduation.
BECKY, who makes it a quintet.

HALFWAY THROUGH THE TUNNEL

ONE

A WALL OF MARGARETS

YOU AIN'T GONNA ANSWER, HUH? I said, how are you, doc? Well, shit . . . I'm terrific. I heard you sniffle. You have a cold? Maybe I'll just take a snooze here; I've been up since five a.m. I could use a nap. Want to prescribe some tranquilizers for me, doc?

Did you really think I was on a withdrawal trip on Tuesday in the *group*? You asked me if I was taking any drugs, remember? I was shaking. That wasn't drugs, doc. That was rage! Frustration!

Talking to Margaret's like talking to Jeff. Nutty as hell talking to a patient in group therapy when it's just like talking to my husband. Poor Margaret. It's pretty awful with her mother having been in the looney bin. That was the only time Margaret was ever real. When she talked about her mother. Oh, I don't give a shit about Margaret.

I'm just really tired. I'm tired of all the games. All of it. And it's hard to stop the tears because of all my sads. Well, nothing to say, doc. Nothing. How'd I get to this place? I don't remember opening this door. When was it— a hundred years ago you said I was in a neurotic blister. Well, it's popped and big boils are happening.

And I've been coming here a long time and I ain't got nothing to show Jeff for it. He's spent a lot of money and there's nothing to show. Instead of getting better, I'm getting worse. I'm just terrible to live with. He's right. I don't like living with me either. The only one I'm half-way decent to is our goddamn kid, and then I feel like shit because Gil loves me like I'm really nice to him.

25

So I don't know what I'm doing here. I can't seem to scream my way out of this tunnel; I can't shake my way out of it; I can't booze my way out of it; or dope my way out of it. There's no way out of it! And I'm sick to death of it. . . .

What I'm most sick of is to have to pay to talk to somebody. And that's such a rotten indictment of me and the whole . . . of everything else. I can't stand it. Stop the bad tears, doc. Make them go and not come back.

Once in awhile, I'll rap with my neighbor, Nancy, about the kids. Except for her, there's not one other adult besides you and the women in the *group* that I talk to. And I don't know why. I don't know why I can't get any answer that doesn't say I'm crazy. Or lazy. Or some awful indictment! Now I know you've told me I'm carrying more than my part of the load. Well, what am I supposed to do about that? Jeff won't get pissed at you and call you names.

NO, NO, buddy, he won't call you names. He calls me names. You know what he said the other night? He said, oh God, Pammie, I ought to be in therapy. And you know there's a zillion reasons that he won't go. One of the reasons is that I'm going twice a week. And the money's flowing out and it ain't flowing in. I sense it clearly that he needs therapy and because of comments you've made, I feel you think so, too.

He won't do it, doc. He won't do it. He hates shrinks. He hates you. He hates Gladstun. Did I ever tell you that Jeff was in analysis with Dr. Gladstun for about four years, and after Jeff finished was when I began therapy with him? Imagine going to the same shrink as my husband! Anyway, he hates Gladstun. He hates himself. He's about as suicidal as I am and that leaves Gil with nobody. He's in worse shape than I am except I scream a lot and walk around with a long face. Shit like that. And he just ties himself in knots, and more knots and more knots. Why are we doing this to ourselves? I don't know. I just don't know. I don't understand. It's really dumb. There's a whole lot we got going and we're just pushing it down the sewer. And doing a lot of pushing. I don't understand it.

There's not a damn thing he and I have to talk about, except everything, and then we wind up not having one single thing to say to each other. I don't know. The whole thing is just piled on his head. All this survival is fine; make a living; make a living. So we have a kid, you know, and the kid's cross-eyed. So it takes a whole lot out of us to get his eyes fixed. Twists our guts around with worry. Now the kid's got allergies, and he's got to go to the doc once a week to get his lousy shots.

And we got a dog. You know what kind of dog we got? A sweet, lovable, crippled dog who's now at the vet's for a whole week with a goddamn cast on his leg.

I mean the whole thing. It's a lot. . . . I've lost my sense of humor about it all. It's not even funny anymore. It's just sickening.

Some people would say it's nothing. They'd say we're lucky. People have kids who are Mongolian idiots or have muscular dystrophy and all kinds of shit like that. We got a healthy, bright little boy whose snout clogs up, that's all. Comes by it by his genes on his mother's side.

Jeff keeps rapping about vasectomies. Well, why the hell doesn't he go get one so I can get rid of this goddamn plug that gives me so much trouble! Let him go get his nuts cut. He's talking vasectomy . . . he gives me this story for months. He keeps talking about this stupid thing. Well, I finally said, okay, go; I don't want any more kids.

And then suddenly . . . suddenly out of nowhere he tells me he has varicose veins in his testicles. Whatever the hell ever that is . . . I never heard about that before . . . ever. It's . . . you know . . . so surgery becomes a little bit more than just a slicing procedure, pflitt, pflitt. It's a little bit more. Now he tells me it's a little bit more. I'll go and have my tubes tied. What do I give a shit? I get to go. Go. Yea, go instead of him.

You know Cindy? I told you about Cindy, my sister's

oldest kid; she's been here from New York. Well, she's not going to be here very long, maybe till the end of next month. I'm missing her already, and I don't even know for sure when she's leaving.

Was it so awful for Cindy to go to the theater? You'd think she got syphilis from Jeff's reaction. He moaned about her spending money that wasn't even his. Oh, maybe Jeff just was poor too long and he thinks poor. I just did the checkbook today. We're down to zero. It's true. I don't care. I hate the rotten money. He wanted a shaver for Christmas, so I got him this shaver. The best electric shaver I could find. But I did more. You know what I did? I was thinking about it for a long time. I went to a really neat store and I plunked down $140.00 cash and I bought him the most beautiful winter coat in the whole world. So maybe he'll go for a walk with me.

I'm tired of this rage, doc.

It's goddamn cold in *there,* in the *group* therapy room. How can two adjoining rooms be so different in temperature? This room . . . the *individual therapy* room, with this . . . this couch I plunk down on to cry is much warmer. Why don't you have one big room, so the *group* could meet *here* where it's warm instead of *there.* Maybe with one room you'd charge less and Jeffy would not bitch as much about money.

And that stupid Margaret. She's a wall. Well, Jeff's a wall! I'm tired of playing his mother, I'm tired of playing Cindy's mother and Gilly's mother. I want to be a little girl for awhile. I want somebody to take care of me for awhile.

But if I let them care for me, see, there's a little voice in me saying cut out that shit. Play grownup for a change. It's just, just boring and the trouble is I lost my sense of humor in the past few days. None of it's even funny. None of it. Not now . . . anymore.

Besides that, I gained two pounds. I weighed in Tuesday after the *group.* I waited until the ladies had gone down the elevator and left the building. I gained two whole pounds

28

Well, terrific. I went home and ate a bag of donuts. Maybe the drug store scale was two pounds off. Yea, that's it. The scale was off.

You know what I'm tired of? I'm tired of being the Rock of Gibraltar to everybody. Is it something in me that I can't get people to help me? That I can't dump on them the way they dump on me? I have to pay to dump it. I know I'm not alone in the world. There are six other women or five women in the *group* and a zillion other people in the world paying for it too. That's why I hate the stupid world.

There was a good article in the paper today. I don't remember his name. By some British guy. He reviewed that best seller. Number one on the list, I think. The guy was good. The American way. How did he say it? Something about how we think in terms of atrocity. I thought, well, hell, yea. This guy's got us; he's got us right there on the line. He pinned us right to the wall. I thought it was terrific. But it didn't shake me out of it.

If I could only measure time. Maybe I haven't been in therapy long, but it seems like a long time. . . . Your turn at bat, doc. Come on, doc, talk to me. Just because I didn't listen the last time you talked doesn't mean I won't now. Bat again. Everybody gets two turns at this game. Come up to bat again, doc. Somebody just broke his elbow— me. . . . I need a pinch hitter . . . you're mad at me because of the way I respond to Jeff, aren't you?

He hates shrinks. He thinks you're phoney. He thinks you don't give a shit except making bread. I'm sure you feel he's wrong, and you can think that way. He thinks all shrinks are only after bread. He's always thought that. The guy's got a B.A. in psychology, right? He knows where it's at. People become shrinks because then they're the judges and nobody can judge them. He compared you once to some guy who works for NIMH.

The guy at NIMH is a dedicated man, according to Jeff. Busts his guts to help people. And you don't accommodate yourself at all to anybody. That's what Jeff says. I happen to agree with him. But it doesn't make much difference because I happen to like you, and I think you can help me. Jeff thinks so too. He has these two things. Then there's a third thing. He ain't seeing anything tangible with me. You tell me that you, the shrink, see changes. But he, the husband, says no. That's what he says. Resounding NO's. Maybe the reason the no is so loud and heavy is because he is seeing changes, but he doesn't like what he sees. Maybe that's it.

Well, shit, if that's it, I don't like the change either! It hurts. It hurts to grow. I can't. Too goddamn painful. It's just terrible. It's just meaningless. Where does that leave me then? More pain than before and it's getting worse. It's not worth the hurt. No.

Listen, Jeff was afraid of my coming here from the very beginning. He told one of our friends that. He said, she's gonna go there. And she's gonna leave me. He thinks of you as this big sheik with your bored women . . . neurotic women. The harem. That's what he calls the *group*. The harem. And he says every goddamn shrink's solution to everything is divorce. Except that's what he's always talking about himself. He's part shrink, you know. And part Jewish mother, too.

Did you know Jeff was a bastard? Not that kind . . . well, yea, that kind too. Who isn't? But he's both kinds of bastards. Born to a mother that didn't marry for whatever reason. So she had this kid and what did she do? Rejected him. And he was adopted by this couple, see, and about two years later he wasn't their kid anymore. The welfare people said he was not treated right, so they took him back and placed him in a foster home. And these great foster parents rejected him too. Three for three. The foster parents were the best, though. Jeff considers them his parents.

My parents rejected him because he wasn't a Jewish lawyer, or doctor . . . because he wasn't Jewish. I know if he were Jewish, though, they'd have rejected him any way . . . that's . . . his way is to. . . . So where does he work? He's only one of a handful of Americans in the whole stupid organization of thousands. So he's suspicious they are suspicious of him. Great. What the hell's he expect? Oh . . . five for five . . . a zillion for a zillion rejections. And he doesn't like the changes in me, doc. Understand what I'm trying to say?

Oh, listen doc, it's all me right now. I can't tell you about Jeffy. I don't know him anymore. I don't know. I don't know what's happening. I know the whole hemisphere and computer is sitting on his head. I know they bug him everyday. Come here. Go there. Come. Go. Things are blowing up in Nam . . . Cambodia. He's going to Japan in January. He sends Bob here; Larry there. He'd send anybody anywhere so he won't go.

I don't know if I said this before, but with Jeff I feel like a kid with her parents. The parent says, I've given you this, I've given you that, I've wiped your a's and blown your nose and given you all the toys and the whole bit. And the kid says yea, but *where were you?* And that's how I feel. Jeff gives me the house, and the shrink and the whole thing. But where is he? Is guilt all there ever is? I mean it sure is familiar to me. God knows I never let the familiar go. That must be what's happening.

And my sister, Sara. You know how I fought with Grace that day in the *group* when Grace said my sister was dumping Cindy on me. No, no, Sara's not dumping Cindy on me, I told Grace, but she was right. Sara is a putrid piece of shit. Jeff's been telling me that for ten years and it's true. You should see the letters she writes to her own kid. It's awful. Cindy's just blooming. She's like a bud just opening up since she got here with us. She's been here—what— two weeks, three weeks, not even that. The whole school's turned on to her. She's sold a zillion of her drawings. Made forty bucks in two weeks. All these people; she's lost weight; she's stopped wearing her Resurrection City overalls. She looks terrific. She's great and open and real. Even her biology teacher is flipping over her. And this woman, her mother, my disgusting sister, writes these god-awful letters. OOOH, what absolute crap.

My sister's just vile. My sister's a piece of shit. She always has been. And she hates my guts. She never even told Cindy that I had a master's degree in philosophy. Cindy about flipped when she learned that about me.

Y'know . . . in the last *group* session, I was intimidated by Helen and Grace. I blew the whole session. I blew it. I just was so frustrated Tuesday. Frustrated at me that I couldn't get across what I wanted to say. What . . . what bugs me is that, uhm . . . it sounded to me like they're saying that the answer to everything is to split. I'm not interested in splitting. I'm interested in getting myself together, getting Jeff and me together, and uhm . . . I don't want to split. I can't help it if they are married to schmucks and divorce is the answer for them. But . . . uhm . . . I, I, I . . . somehow I can't get that across, it seems. I felt really bad about the whole thing. Like a barrier *is* between those ladies and me.

I think . . . this is gonna sound like a back-off, but I found in earlier experiences that the more I dug in with the relationships right there in the *room* . . . about how I felt about each of those ladies, the more it helped me in hearing Jeff. In . . . in my relationship with him. And I feel I'm not digging in enough. That I haven't dug in enough for a really long time now in my relationship with Helen or Grace. Or the others. I chicken out and I'm sorry.

I'm being controlled by my own fears. Goddamn it, doc, I don't know how to get out of it. I don't know what to do. How do I work it?

There's always the fantasy in my head of split. Quit. Quit therapy. Quit Jeff. I don't know what that means—quit Jeff. I mean I don't know what I would do to go away. You know, to get in the car and go away.

I'm more scared of the painful moments than anything. To look into the future. And I don't mean future far away. I mean future tomorrow. Next day. I had a lot of fantasy talks with Jeff this week and what I wanted to say was . . . uhm. . . . To change the emphasis. I don't know if that's the same as priorities. These fantasy conversations with Jeff sort of become where life is. I tend to get—I don't know about my behavior—but in my head, I tend to get absolute. I'm afraid, so afraid, that *I'm not me* with Jeff, that I'm someone from my past or his past. I'm afraid the last ten years with us has been one pack of shit. One huge lie, from that point of view.

I'm sort of just talking to myself now. That's how I conduct these horrible dialogues in my head. . . . Start now for something else. I, uhm . . . it's why I can't talk about splitting with the ladies in the *group*. What I'm really scared of is what if I start getting healthy. Suppose I stop being mother and shrink and get healthy. Suppose then, across the board, I don't dig this man anymore, for whatever my mixed-up reasons. So here's the abyss, and I don't know what's across that chasm over there.

See, for me . . . I get mixed up at this point. Uhm, where the real person, the whole person comes and says, look, this is how I see life. This is how I want to be. This is where I dig it. You want to come this way? With me? The difference between that and the domineering put-down bitch my mother was . . . that kind of image . . . look Izzy, you're a schmuck, and you can't earn a goddamn dime, so I'm moving outta this house and I'm going to work. . . . So in here, when I'm rapping with you, I can see those differences. Jeff's strong. I want that. I don't want a namby-pamby little boy like my sister's married to.

Ten years ago, when we got married and I started pulling crap, I wanted somebody to slap me in the face and say, knock it off. Okay, that's what I wanted ten years ago. I don't want it now. Ten years ago there were physical slaps. It's not like that anymore. Now it's verbal slaps, it's psychological shit—no more grapefruits in the face. Who needs it? The old me needed it. I want to say the real me. Will the real Pammie please stand up? Goddamn son-of-a-bitch, he's driving me crazy. I have enough crazies of my own. You can't have it both ways, Jeffy boy. You can't have it both ways. I'm fed up with it. . . . Well, if I were somebody else, I'd say, you're fed up with it—split. But this is not some ass-hole I'm married to. This is a groovy human being. And I'm on the right track to make it groovy for us.

These past two weeks, while Jeff's been away, I had more time to think. Read three books. There have only been a few moments when I missed him. I can look around. See things. What is that painting of a soup can? I have only one ticket. Whenever, ten, twenty years from now, I'm gonna be in the dirt. They're going to throw dirt on my face. And what am I going to do about it between now and then? When I think that way it's scarey. I don't often face it like that. And not very long when I do. I want me to radiate out. Out into my painting, my writing, my loving. Into the rapping. There are people who say to me, I'm so real. Cindy says to me, you're so real. She knows all the garbage about me and all the shit I take from Jeff. Somehow maybe my reality gets out. I see me as a series of circles. Radiating circles. And I think some of those circles come from the middle. Some come from god knows where, but some come from the middle. I think some of those that come out from the middle are the real me. Some have come out from me to you; a lot of it's come out to Jeffy. It scares him shitless when that real stuff comes out. I know it scares me because I can't make the circles radiate out when I want them to. I suppose maybe when I start fooling around with canvas and stuff, that's what's so strange about it. I guess I'm frightened of the real. That's why I won't take my paintings to the gallery, or the writing to the publisher. My biggest fantasy is that—to discover my center and BE in the world. That's my most private, in so far as I can describe it, place where I'm at.

Two

TWO CHRISTMAS CARDS

I PLANNED TO GIVE YOU A CHRISTMAS CARD, and I didn't do it. Then I planned to tell you what was in it and I'm not sure I can say it. So I'm going to start with the unconscious and tell you about a dream. You know, it really ought to be dark today. The sun shouldn't be shining. I dreamed about you last week and, uhh, and that was one of the reasons I was sort of weird in the *group*.

I was in this big house. Do you have to have that music piped in here? I was in this big house, see; I was sick; I was lying in bed in this huge big, rich, wealthy house. And I had a lot of children. And you came to visit me. Because I was sick, right? But you looked sort of funny 'cause you had these funny clothes on. You had, uhm . . . cut-off Levis, like Bermuda length, and a shag and then you had on this, uhm, midriff, uh, Levi jacket with fringes. Long fringes. And you came in and you lay down on the bed with me. And I said, uhh, something like, that's gonna look funny, doc. It's really weird. I was really sick, like—like in those old movies. It seemed like it was an old movie. Uhh, where those mothers . . . are always withering away from some terrible disease, and they're invalids. And we rapped for awhile. You were very friendly. And then I showed you around this big house. Introduced you to my family. Lots of . . . maybe not lots, but more than what I've got. And, uh, older. Oh, I don't know, it was really weird. I've forgotten it now.

I wanted so much to remember it, so much to go . . . One of those dreams I go back into, and I've been living in it for a week. It was weird. And, uhh. . . . Yea, it was very

35

real. Terribly very real. Uhh, I've been living in this fantasy about you, and I don't like it.

I'm in that classical place I suppose they write about in the books. I don't know the terms for it, but I'm sure you do. I don't like it. It's not right. It's out of boredom, out of fear that I'm in this place. And, because you're the only other adult male who's handy, who's in my life at the present time. And there isn't anybody else to fantasize about. And because things are so peculiar between Jeff and me. And so . . . he's home today. He told me that he drinks because of me. Jeff told me that he told you that, that one day he took my appointment. He told me he wasn't putting the guilt on me. And I haven't been very loving to him in recent weeks. And I can't seem to get through *why* to him or maybe even to me. And so I go into these fantasies and having that dream about you really wiped me out.

He says to me, why do you scream at Gil and me and everybody? And I said, it's rage. I told him he's not the only one who has rage. Maybe this is the first time in my life I've recognized it. I told him how I respond to Margaret in the *group*. I said I shake. I shake with rage when I talk with her, because talking with her is like talking with you. With you, Jeff.

Anyway, doc. I want to dig into this thing with you. And it's really scarey and really embarrassing, and I want to do it and get out of it.

And I was going to send—give you this Christmas card that says:

Dear Ann Landers,

I've been seeing this man twice a week for several months. Once in the company of others and once a week alone. He's married and has kids, and he likes dogs. I'm worried that the attraction is purely physical because he looks like André Previn. Do you think I should see a psychiatrist? Merry Christmas.

I knew you would laugh. I knew you would like that Christmas card. And maybe because of that I never did write it down.

So there you are—Merry Christmas, doc. That's my gift to my shrink. Grace said that sometime when I come in, I should ask to see her Christmas card to you. Do you know that I hugged her out in the hall? Do you know that Jeff asks about Grace—how is Grace? It's just really weird.

Hey, get me out of this place, will you? I've never experienced this before, really, with other shrinks. And it's, uhh—with Dr. Rosenberg I did it vicariously through Chuck, according to him, and I still dig Chuck. Oh, we got a Christmas card from Chuck. He wrote it; he's so funny. I wrote them a letter and, uhh, I told you—he used to tease me a lot about being in therapy when we lived in New York. I said I'm with this shrink now, and he was not to laugh. He wrote back and said:

> Dear Jeff and Pam,
>   HO HO HO . . .
> That's not a laugh at the psychiatrist,
> but I did permit myself a grin.

He's really groovy. He sent pictures of Lana, his wife, and the kids, and there weren't any of him. So I wrote a Christmas card back and said, is it because you're getting fat that there were no pics of you? I'm sure he's not; he's gorgeous. What he did send was a picture of his son who was born since we left there. I think his name was Alexander Scott or Scott Alexander. Anyway I love the name Alexander. He's a funny looking kid, and they had a picture of him that was kind of interesting to Gil. He was watering the lawn with his spritzer, and he was totally naked. He's really cute.

I miss those people. I miss . . . see, uhm. Like last night we went over to Nancy's and Paul's house for, uhm, a little Christmas dinner. She's so up tight. Paul's really neat. But she's like Margaret, she doesn't understand flip. Remember that, in the *group* session on Tuesday? You know I always start to shake when I talk to Margaret. But Jeffy teases Nancy, and she doesn't know how to take it. He says, why do these people get up tight? And I said to him, look here, I said to him what I said to Margaret, and I told him that I said it to her, that flip keeps you from going under.

And people we've always held very dear to us always understood about what flip means; they always understood, like. . . . Do you recall Dr. Dieterdoff, my professor, who used to say in class to us, you can't think seriously about any of this stuff for more than ten minutes or you go under? So that's why people laugh when they hear about car accidents. And when they think about the bomb, they have to laugh. That was the context of it at the time. 'Cause he understood about flip. And, uhm, look, I'm not getting out of this place.

I'm beating around the bush. All these things are important stuff for me to say, but I gotta stop going from one thing to another. And I gotta quit trying to find the becauses and just, uhh, just feel. That's really new to me. Just say, hey, today, this is how I feel. I mean you saw . . . those women in the *group* wipe me out . . . you saw how when Irene told about tying the ribbon around whatever his name is, around his penis, that I didn't know what to do with it.

I'm not used to people being able to say, look, I feel shit today, or I feel loving and scared today. And just there it is. I don't . . . you know that's real existence right there, and this whole rage is new. The need for mystery and adventure—that's not new. I mean the mystery and adventure— that's all the fantasy about you. I mean I've been there all my life. Fantasizing. And running away from it.

I ran away from it the last couple of weeks by eating like a pig. Getting as fat and ugly as I can to get away from you, from Jeff, from my own fantasies, to get away from fucking.

None of it's real. I've lost how to be real. I know what's

38

real and what's not; what's hostile and what's not; what's aggressive and what's not. That's something I know. What I don't know is how to *BE* real.

It is not a new place; I've been in this place before, too, but I—uhh—look, I don't like it. It's just that simple. I feel indifferent. I feel a funny kind of strength, but there are all these rotten manifestations. I don't know if they're manifestations. I . . . I . . . I . . . I try to cut off the games, and now I can't tell if I'm successful or unsuccessful, and that's why it's so rotten I can't tell which is which. I feel different, but I don't know what it is.

Something in the back of my head is telling me you're about to say that you're happy that I feel crappy. And there's something in the back of my head that says that. But that's really weird.

Why is it that I can comfort my son, my niece, even sometimes people in the *group,* but it stops dead when it comes to my husband?

And Jeff was going to send you a Christmas card, too, and here's his card:

> Dear Dr. Becky,
>   Please clear up my wife's cunt,
> so, oh, so she'll love me.
> > > > Merry Christmas.

Something like that.

How come I can't comfort him? He's in such rotten shape. Maybe because I'm the reason for it. I thought if I could get over fantasizing about you, or stop thinking about some other fantasy object, I could approach him. Really, maybe that would help me. It's not that I want to screw with you, or make love with you. It's just, uhh, oh—I suppose it's the classic thing, because we can laugh, you know, you got a nice sense of humor. And, uhh, because I, it's like, uhh. . . . It's the same thing as when I like to baby-sit for my friend's little baby. I do the baby thing with him, and it's okay because I go home in a couple hours, and I don't have to wipe his ass and blow his nose for the rest of my life.

So I can come here and rap twice every week. I don't want to keep coming to therapy all my life. I don't want to have to pay for friends all my life. I don't want to keep responding to Jeff the way I do to Margaret. I mean he and I have touched base, but we keep losing it. I mean we've touched base verbally a couple of times in the last week or so, but, God, we keep losing it. And, uhh . . . oh I'm just so tired. I'm so bored. I'm so god-awful bored.

See, it's just a horrible vicious circle. I can't talk to him through that alcoholic fog. I just can't. I won't. I hate it, I told him so. And he tells me he drinks at home. He doesn't on his trips. He drinks at home AT HOME!

Now, which me is he getting away from? The little Jewish girl he married who made him laugh eleven years ago? The hostile bitch? The painter? I don't know. The mother? Maybe it didn't all start then. But Gil became the catalyst. When I became a mother. He's sleeping with somebody else's mother.

He feels like an object, like we use him. It kills him to buy himself something. Our car died. It killed him to buy himself that new car. He'll go until he has twenty thousand holes in his shoes before he'll buy himself a pair of shoes. I can't handle that whole *you talk* thing inside him.

I'm like the only link that's good and true and beautiful— like we used to say in Philosophy 1-0-1.

I used to dig that. Why don't I dig it anymore? See it's . . . I . . . I don't want . . . I have a lot of crummy attributes from my own mother, but I have similar attributes to his mother. At least I've shown them in recent weeks, probably because of Cindy.

Give it all out to the wrong people. That's what Muriel did to Jeff all of his life. She still does it. Some foster mother! She'll always do it. She always gave the love and affection of any emotion the woman was capable of feeling

40

to anybody but Hugh and Jeff and her husband. Hugh was Jeff's foster brother. Don't laugh. Foster's thicker than water. God, she even gave it to me. Never to them. It's just a goddamn empty void in Jeff that I can't fill up. And then I start to act like Muriel does. I give it to Gil, I give it to Cindy, I give it to you, I give it to Grace; I'm sick of it. I'm sick of this whole stupid life. I'm sick of Richard Nixon and all his shit. You know I don't read the newspapers. Jeff reads it. He reads all that bad news.

I don't want to hear that bad news. I don't care if the whole world belches and then blows up. There's not a goddamn thing I can do about it. I don't want to hear about it while I'm still here. I want to keep the shit from seeping in the walls. Just shovel against the tide. We're all living in Holland. All of us have our little fingers in little holes in the dike, except it's not precious life-giving ocean that's coming in. It's garbage, it's filth. Lies.

You know it's really bad. My sister sent me some bath oil when Cindy came. Cindy brought it. It was bath oil that Myrna had introduced to me. And I use it. Everytime I put it on, I think about Myrna, and I really shouldn't use it 'cause I really shouldn't think about her. She's been dead two years now. Because I loved her and she was my dearest friend and because she's dead, I shouldn't think about her. I've got to tell you about Myrna some day.

Just like watching that movie of Robert Kennedy the other night. Yea. Yea. He was really terrific. I always thought that he was a creep. Well, yea, so it's a propaganda film. He's probably really terrific. Well, so what? Are we going to vote for a dead man now?

It's awful. All these goddamn things running into my head. It's awful. On the other hand, I think I really groove on it, I really dig it. I love being in this stupid place. Obviously, or I'd get the hell out. Didn't Freud say people seek pleasure? Well, like Jeff said, he hasn't sought pleasure for years. Really, neither have I.

That brings me back to you. I haven't done or said any-

41

thing about it, with all the shit I've poured out. And I don't want to dream about you. Please tell my unconscious to quit. Besides, you looked very silly in that outfit.

No, you didn't, you looked very nice. In fact, it was sort of funny, 'cause while you looked silly, you also looked nice. And you didn't feel self-conscious. You were Mr. Hippy, and you looked really cute . . . yea, you were. I don't know why the outfit. I don't really understand that. But it was really funny. I supppose . . . you know how sometimes I get up off this couch and go across the room and sit in a chair, and you plop down on this stupid couch? Well, that's what you did in the dream. You just plopped down on the bed like that. Uhm. My reaction was the same as it is in here—you're making me crazy, doc, what are you doing? Well, I guess you were just being real. That's what makes me crazy—I don't know. When people are real. It does, does tend to make me feel. . . . When I say *makes me crazy*—that phrase, it's, uhh, oh, it's not . . . I don't know what to do with it. When I don't know what to do with anything, that's when I say *makes me crazy*. That's how I . . . those are the words I use to describe the feeling. I don't know what to do then. I'm shaky right now.

You know, a long time ago, we lived in Boston and I was in therapy with Rosenberg. I had a dream. We were going to see *Marat Sade* and a few days before I didn't really know too much about the dream. I mean about the play. But a few days before I had this very involved dream, one part of which was when I went to see the play. And the crazy people started walking down the aisles. And it wasn't clear whether they were actors playing crazy or whether they were the real crazy people. And they came, and they propped me up with them, and I was marching with them to the looney bin. It was horrible.

Well, goddamn it, we went to see the real play, right? And it was in the round. And the lights were up. And the crazy people started coming down the aisles. Well, it just blew my mind. It was awful. It was exactly like my dream.

42

It was just terrible. We were sitting in the goddamn front row with these loonies. Well . . . I feel like that now. I know that someday you're gonna say—oh, I never promised you a rose garden, lady. No, I don't know where I am now. It's really weird.

I mean now, right this minute. I have this horrible fantasy . . . I don't know if you're taking notes now. I've had this horrible fantasy since you teach at the medical school of, uhm . . . of all these people in white coats standing around your notes or records of me or whatever, with little scalpels waiting for directions of where to cut now—pflitt, pflitt.

Your taking notes doesn't really bother me. It's just a fantasy I have. I just, well, uhm, a little bit . . . it's like another dream I had. It was interpreted twenty thousand different ways. It's not a dream I like to recall. I've never really had a satisfactory interpretation of it. It's all about being inside, trying to get out. I'm in that little note pad saying, hey, guys, all the people you're ever gonna see in your little rooms, that's all they're asking, guys. I'm in here locked in. Let me out. I'm locked in this note pad, and let me out.

What a *group*. That *group*. I wasn't even there in that *group* last Tuesday. I was there, but I wasn't. You know what I was feeling; I'm just jealous of Irene. I know it's wrong, and she's in the practical bind and all that. Whatever she's feeling for her lover right now is, uhh . . . I'm just jealous of it. I want to feel that way about Jeffy. But she can't feel it for her own husband either.

I was really disappointed when I sat in the shrink chair in the *group* Tuesday and nothing happened. I thought you would have left a little bit of egg on there for somebody. Did you feel different sitting in Grace's chair? Everybody's looking for a little magic. There ain't none. Today's Christmas Eve. It's really weird today. I have another fantasy. The other fantasy is that you weren't my shrink and that you and your wife would come over on Christmas Eve to have a drink. And that gets me back to the same old thing.

43

Could you write me a prescription, doc? You never have drawn that picture of me. This is nice paneling, you know? It's better than your lousy pictures. Looks like a large tit right there. See that curly thing there? That whorl is one rather large tit, I'd say. You know I haven't painted in a long time. I don't know what I'm waiting for. I suppose I'm waiting for a painting to appear. It has to appear first in my gut. Then I open up the gut and pour it on the canvas and close up the gut again. Like that crazy Japanese who cut his head off or cut his gut out or whatever he did. That really impressed me, that story. The man really believed in his principle, bla, bla, bla. Ohhh. I wonder if it's as hard to be an ant as it is to be a human? Do you suppose ants with crazies ask ant shrinks that about humans?

Oh, yea, ants got it really set up. Unless of course you're a worker. That would be me. A worker. You saw that man on TV, din'cha? Told about ants. Anyway I'm coming back as a porpoise. Absolutely. Well, why don't you go ahead and handle that dream, doc . . . now doc . . . come on. Now man. Come on. Do it. We got ten minutes left. I gotta get outta there. No, it's not—go on. Help me to get outta this place, will ya? Maybe I fragmented the dream so beautifully you can't do much with it. Try.

Rosenberg used to say, tell me your dream again, twenty minutes later. All I can tell you is the feeling. It was really nice . . . good feeling. It was just, uhm, it wasn't much different from the feeling I feel in here in private sessions. Uhm. When you plopped down on that bed and I said you don't look good, doc, you kind of did one of your laughy numbers, or flip numbers, and said something like, how are ya? Just really friendly. And the idea that you had that funny outfit on, it was just . . . I guess it was like you trusted me. I wasn't gonna laugh at you. You weren't a clown. But it was part of the flip, part of the funny, like when I dreamed about Rosenberg, you know, portly stomach, and his tie with chicken soup stains, and his jacket, and his shorts below his knees, and garters. You know, that was a clown. That was putting him down. You and this flip thing, the funny Levi outfit, with your bare midriff and the fringe, I don't know. You're real and with it. It's so funny. I can see it, and I'm right in there. But it's so hard to say what happened. I just felt invalidy. Powerless. And happy to see you. I felt about you the way I felt about Chuck, only more. It's just always nice to see him and be with him, and rap and exchange sarcasms and sillies and just be really friendly. Does that give you enough? Can you explain the dream now? Huh?

You're kidding. I thought it was a classic thing and you could find a label. Page 233. Right out of Sigmund's collected dream material. The dream's got worth. It's got trust and liking and sexual things. Let it out, doc, 'cause it's starting to get me.

I, well . . . I . . . I try to translate that into sexual fantasies. That's what bugs me, not the friendlies. See, I wanna feel, I suppose, friendly and sexual and all of that. What is that? It's all life's force. I wanna feel that feeling about Jeff. I want us to have that. I want us to be, uhh . . . what I just said I felt about you in that dream I wanna feel about him. That's what bugs me. I mean if I didn't really like him, if I didn't really love him, I wouldn't cry so goddamn much about it. I do feel this pain, but I can't . . . somehow I can't show it to him. Just like I couldn't say it to Irene, yea. Maybe because, maybe because I don't know . . . either I can't feel it, or I don't believe this pain, or I don't want to hear about it. Too selfish to hear about it. I don't know what it is. It's true I don't want to hear about this pain. It's just too overwhelming. It's just too much. It's pulling him under. I guess I'm just a strong enough ego not to want to be pulled under, too. It's so. How can I pull him up? And don't give me the jazz about my taking care of his problems too, and all that stuff.

This man is my life, and I don't know how to tell him that anymore. It's just god-awful. How do I tell him without my going under? That's what I'm afraid of. I want to say

45

yea, yea, I know, I know, I know, and then he's gonna say, get into this mess with me. I don't want to go in there. I don't want to go into that awful whirlpool where he is. And god knows it's a strong one, and so I've been pulling away and pulling away, and not feeling and not loving, and not screwing and not anything. I don't want in there. But I want him to get out, and he hasn't got you to help him. And he's too afraid, too ashamed, too . . . he won't let you help him. And that's where it is.

Well, I'll tell you something, doc, you're a good shrink 'cause I never knew that was gonna come out.

Yes, you're right. This goddamn fucking couch is really magical.

THREE

TO THE MUSEUM WITH LOVERING

YOU REALLY OUGHT TO LET YOUR hair grow. In the back a little. She's right. It's freezing in here. She talked to me—that girl who sees you just before me. She's really pretty. Wow, she's doing lots better. She smiles more.

Well, doc, what shall we talk about today? Uhm, first I'll start with a message from Jeff, who says:

> I relinquish control to you, Dr. Becky,
> As one chauvinist to another.

Okay, that's the end of his message.

What did he mean? What did . . . uhm, oh, well, I don't know what he meant. I can tell you what I think he meant. It's about therapy. Well, I was going to come here and quit, because Jeff is envious of my being in therapy. Two, he's not sure he's going to get anything out of my being in therapy. So far he hasn't. How are those for starters?

He also said . . . yesterday was a real break in the muddy waters. We had a real nice afternoon. He said, uhm . . . I said some things to him the night before that he'd apparently given a great deal of thought. And he said, uhm, I'm probably not quoting him directly, but he said, I thought about what you said, meaning me, and you are getting well.

It was really a nice thing for him to say. So it's, ahh, it's with this hand that he is giving and with that hand he is taking back. It's . . . it's, ahh, a kind of a positive, but it's also a negative. I mean . . . I see it as a negative because my response was control to me. I said, you mean

47

to me. He said, no, to Becky. And I said, as one chauvinist to another.

I mean that sort of left . . . here I am, sort of a nice little ping-pong ball between two pricks. I didn't dig that part of it, but the underneath part of it is okay. I just would hope that . . . to cut out that bad stuff.

So what! You never know! And, uhm, after yesterday afternoon I thought you were right about what you said in the *group* on Tuesday. That, uhm, I don't know what you said—something like, there are ways out of the muddy waters. I didn't . . . I . . . I didn't believe it then. I believed it some yesterday and I'm just sort of teetering on this little fence that's stuck in the middle of the muddy waters now. It can go either way. It is really tenuous.

On Tuesday . . . was really neat. It was a really neat thing because of what Helen said again. Just great. And real. Some of those women in the *group!* And then, when we left the session, the elevator was really crowded, and Grace asked me if we'd celebrated Chanukah, and I said yea, both. 'Cause Jeff's not Jewish. And, uhh . . . uh, some banter happened because I was really out of it. And, uhh, the elevator stopped at some place, and some guys were gonna get on, and Grace said, sorry, fellas, and instead of pushing the close button to close the elevator, I kept holding onto the open door button. It was really funny, and everybody laughed.

But as I walked out of the building, Helen and Maxine . . . uhm, especially Helen said some . . . some really nice things, and she said, I know it's really difficult where you are to talk about whatever it is. She said, I have been there, and Maxine agreed she'd been there. She said, but I hope next week you really will try, because we like you a lot; we care. And it was just . . . it was really something else!

I don't know. I just touched her arm. I'm not much on touching people. It scares me. And . . . I . . . I just sort of squeezed her arm and went in the car and cried for about

48

five or six minutes. A lot. Dropped a lot of salt. And for the rest of that day, I was preparing a letter in my head to give to you to read to them because I was gonna quit. And then what happened Wednesday night was . . . we got hold of this hash, and we smoked . . . some hash.

Now, I didn't really smoke it. I just faked it. But I know I used that moment to get through to Jeffy because you can on that stuff. I never told you why I almost cancelled on Tuesday. The Christmas scene was so awful, just so awful, God, it was an alcoholic fog, just uckk. It was ghastly. And Cindy apparently was . . . or Jeff felt she was kind of a catalyst, just the way Gilly was when he was born. A catalyst for shit that was already there, and Jeff was saying, he was talking about her strong ego structure, and that I get sucked in. And the family, and Jewish, and, oh, just all of it—schhukkkk—just came down like an avalanche! And he wasn't gonna . . . he didn't trust her with Gilly; he'd never seen any evidence that she liked Gil and all this shit. And he wasn't gonna let her baby-sit.

See, I had asked her to baby-sit for me Tuesday and I was just gonna take off the whole day and go to the *National Geographic* and see the *Sistine Chapel* reproduction. And so, uhm, when he threw that on me I just . . . I . . . had threatened before to quit or to cancel. And we'd gone around and around as always . . . when he was home. I said, aw, shit. And he said, I'll come home to baby-sit. And I wasn't gonna bear that guilt. The thing always was when I started the *group* . . . it meant less of me for Jeff. He felt threatened.

Then the money thing gets into it. That I was never gonna pay a baby sitter. And I certainly wasn't gonna have him come home from work. On and on. And I just couldn't do it, so I called in and cancelled. And his reaction after I hung up the phone, after talking to your secretary, you know, was like PWHOOO, like a tire about to burst that wasn't gonna burst now 'cause it was losing air. That's how I read it. I might be wrong. For him it was like the

pressure had left. Maybe for me, too. I don't know. I just
. . . I don't . . . I don't really know. I just read in him,
maybe he felt it was a vote for him in some sense. I don't
know. I don't really know. Look, I don't have the words
to describe what I read in him. I just saw a kind of bodily
relaxation.

And the next day, I had this big long talk with Cindy
about the house, responsibility, bla, bla, bla; a really good
rap. And she finally came through, and he finally saw that
evening some evidence of caring for Gilly and so on, and
he said, okay, she can baby-sit. So that's why I came to
the *group.*

Then, Tuesday night, he started smoking this hash, and
I knew he was . . . he was high, and so I was able to say
things I could never, almost never say when he's sober
and get through. And absolutely, categorically never when
he's drunk. I hate what booze does to him. And I told
him . . . he never seemed to understand what I meant
about the rage, even though he lived with rage all his life.
Maybe he can't understand it when somebody else feels it
who didn't have the outside . . . uhh, rotten environment
to produce it. Like his environment was awful.

And so I remem . . . recalled, years ago, in the first years
of our being together, once in awhile . . . He's an incurable
tease, and we would horse around in the bed, and if he
ever held my hands down like this with both my arms
up and back, along side my head, like in the *stick'em up*
position, you know, locked me so that I was totally vulnerable, not really vulnerable, just couldn't move, I had this
instant, instant, INSTANT, rage response. He gave me that
term. I didn't know what it was, I just knew I was going
insane!

You know, I would just immediately go berserk. I'd
begin to sob just immediately. And his having a whole
zillion hours and a degree in psych, he knew it was a rage
response. At least, that's what he labelled it.

So I used that memory when we were in the kitchen,

and I told him, you remember that game when you described that rage response? That's what I'm talking about. And I said a lot of other things. I've said a number of things to him this week, many of which really hurt him. At one moment . . . I mean he just gets so awful, because one minute he's saying really terrible things. And, uhm, and then there might be a moment of silence. And he said, why am I so cruel to you? How often? How much am I cruel to you? And I always bite the bitter bait. Always. Yea. And I said in the most sober voice, eighty-five percent of the time. Well, this man's a statistician, right? You hit him with a number like that, and it was like hitting him with a sledge hammer. And uhm . . . god, it was just awful. I just really hit him. I don't know, I just picked a number. I wanted to pick the most accurate number. I don't have much feel for numbers. But I have never been able to tell him in any way. Anyway that's one of the things I told him, some of the things, I don't remember.

And then I . . . and I guess I got through 'cause yesterday was just so peaceful, so comfortable. Just to sit together. Just . . . just to talk, just to listen. I didn't feel defensive. I thought maybe there's some hope. Maybe I could quit thinking about money shit, and this shit that he dumps on me, and think about what kind of shit I'm producing and work on me, because therapy is available to me. I guess what . . . a . . . one of the things that I do is the rising decibel of my voice when I feel these walls, these bricks start piling between us, and I get like I am right now. I just begin to scream.

This only happened to me once before when I couldn't contain what goes on in the therapy room, within the walls. When I was first in therapy with Kaplin, back when I was in college, and I was so hostile to my mother, I couldn't contain it in the therapy room. I just had to let it drip out, to get it to her. I had to do whatever I could do to get it to her, to let her know I hated her guts. And, uhh, see, I don't, uhh . . . why I couldn't do this in the *group* is that I'm . . . a . . . two reasons. I'm not filled with trust yet for seven other women, and two, I just have such guilt. I don't have guilts about talking about him to you, but talking about him to *them* with their divorces and their shitty husbands and their shitty separations and their affairs, and the whole thing. I just can't handle it yet. It is just too close to the bad rapping of him to Jan. She's the friend I mentioned from New York. Sometime I'll tell you about Jan. Even though those women aren't Jan, none of them are . . . I don't think. So far as I know any of them.

I just never know what's gonna happen on this couch— it's really funny. I just live on this fucking couch day after day. It's weird.

We were having lunch today, and I was sitting . . . I had my hair dryer on, and Jeff said, oh, you're getting all prettied up for Becky, and I said, no, for me. Why don't you come with me, and he said, oh, no. Never. I'm well. . . . And we burst out laughing. It was really a funny joke. Cindy said, I'll come with ya, and I said, no. Once in awhile he calls you by your real name. He prefers Becky.

Yea, some nice things are happening . . . yet . . . I . . . only . . . it's so tenuous, doc, it really is. It scares me. I don't know. You once said something to me—I don't remember the words exactly. Like I wasn't . . . you said, you're not really aware of what your presence does. Was it something like that you once said to me? Hmm? Another thing that's really scaring me is that I'm slowly, just a tiny little bit, becoming aware or admitting to or seeing or whatever the word is, whichever is right, uhm . . . of my power.

Jeff said to me some nights ago, I don't know when it was. He said, you really have the power to relax me. He didn't mean just sexually. And I saw the other night, ya know, that night I just faked the hash, I didn't want that shit. But unless I'm high, when I get high on that stuff, I just really get funny. I just get more of what I am. And it's, uhh, well . . . Jeff just really grooves on it, just really enjoys it. And, ya know, nothing happens if I don't get high. Nobody else laughs and giggles. So I don't really need that stuff 'cause I'm always there anyway. But as I think . . . as I recall that night, need it or not, I used it.

That's right. Real calculated used it. I've never as deliberately and consciously done anything that way before. And sure I've used things, but not that deliberately. I . . . it was, oh . . . I'm grasping at anything, doc. I can't take that booze scene. I just can't. That will put me right under. That's that whirlpool and I'm not going in there. So I'd just as soon the man become a junky. See, I . . . oh . . . I feel really guilty for having just said that. I'm . . . I'm so frightened. I'm on that fence, that tight rope. And nice things are happening, right? Nice things have so often in recent times been just doors open into hell. I'm really scared.

And . . . and the rage is just so much there. I mean . . . the rage on so many things . . . the rage . . . that I can only see people like Helen and Grace in therapy. That I don't know people like that who are friends, who will come over and have coffee and laugh and sit around. People who will *be*. I know I just . . . I just have to get over what the fears are . . . whatever it is that . . . that's keeping me from finding people like that. And being able to . . . to . . . to . . . keep that . . . that separate from my life with Jeff which I hate, too. 'Cause he also wants people. He does and he doesn't. And it's . . . it's just too much.

I . . . he keeps asking, am I crazy? What's wrong with me? He asks me! I don't want the responsibility of answering those questions. I can only maintain a teeney bit of objectivity at that level. I just . . . just sink into my own shit after . . . after a little bit. I don't . . . I don't know, I get into this self-pity thing; no matter what I do, I lose.

He's always hating to go to museums and stuff with Gil, saying Gilly gets sort of bitchy and wants to go here and there. Last Sunday I decided I was gonna go, and he said, okay, I'll go, too. And he found a new way to go to Washington—other than the beltway route. As long as he could do that and not see Route 95 again, that's okay. See, he goes to work on 95, and he won't . . . can't play on 95, too. And we went to the old part with the airplanes and stuff. And I thought, well, he hadn't seen the *Kitty Hawk* and all that junk. Gil and I had been there twenty thousand times, so I just sort of took Gilly around here and there, so Jeffy could read the signs. And then he got on me. He said, let me hold Gilbert's hand, and stuff. We talked about it after, and I said, 'cause it was neat for you to come in and Gil was so delighted that you came to the museum with us. And I wanted you to enjoy it. I didn't want a scene. I didn't want a scene! And I just thought I'd play it as cool as possible and keep Gilly out of his way if he's really looking at something. And he said, you're mothering me again, just like Gladstun said you did.

And you know—where does that put me? That's the trouble having the same shrink back then. He says Gladstun told him that, but Gladstun didn't tell me. There's not a goddamn thing to say! If the kid bugs him and is bitchy, it's my fault. If I keep the kid out of his way, then I'm mothering him. If I try to be there, as I was for Gil today— one of his little friends said . . . was saying something that really hurt Gilly's feelings. He was really sad, and . . . I just . . . you know . . . it's legitimate to mother my kid, isn't it? And he got onto me for it, for creating dependence and shit . . . oh . . . the hell with it. I thought, oh, well, I can't go to therapy and say nice things are happening. The whole shit's piling up again, and then it's settled. It's just like that! It's horrible! It's just horrible.

Sometimes I think I'm like his mother. You know . . . that I give all the affection, all the good stuff to everybody else. To Nancy, to Cindy, to Gil, to the ladies in the *group*, and none to him. In a way that's how I've been, especially sexually. I've . . . I just . . . I don't trust him. I just really know it. It really shows up there. I just . . . it's all . . . there I am. Stop, damn tears. . . .

You know that note you gave me to give to Jeff? Well, he liked your note. He kept it. Took it with him. He thought it was great; he thinks you're really great, and he hates your guts—so there.

That's it. Tune in tomorrow, folks. Remember Helen Trent. See if a woman over thirty-five can find happiness, bla, bla, bla, bla, bla. Except I'm not thirty-five yet.

Well, I think over Christmas, the booze really . . . gets even more in the way. Jeff put away over two half-gallon bottles. Close to that. I didn't have much of it. He was smashed when we went to Nancy's and Paul's for dinner. He and Paul both got smashed. And from then on, with a few breaks for sleeping, I suppose. At least that's how it seemed. It was just awful for all of us. When he's around me, that's all he does. I don't know. It's just a fog. It is all the pain that comes out. It's just all emphasized.

You know, his fucking feelers . . . he's just so . . . I tell him . . . you know . . . he says, you know why I don't like to go to the museum, why it was sort of pleasant Sunday? Because there weren't too many people around. He says, the people. I said, who looks at the people? Don't look at 'em. Just put on some blinders for a change. Suck in your feelers . . . schluupp. Don't lay 'em out there for everybody to step on. Don't. Pull them in. I don't look at anybody in the museum unless it looks like a friendlie. I just don't. I look at the train. . . . I'd like to crawl in that train and just live there for awhile.

He didn't buy a whole bunch of booze for New Year's Eve weekend. Thank god. Last night we were up all night. Goddamn heat went out. Had to wait till five o'clock in the morning for some idiot to bring oil. It was horrible. It was sort of fun up until about three o'clock when I zonked out. And he had to deal with this man by himself who talked, Za, Da, Ba, Ga-Ga-La-La-Dah, you know, one of those who can't speak the language. His DNA came out wrong—NDA—like the way he talks.

It's just amazing . . . I'm . . . uhm . . . from the chemical point of view. I don't know what parts of the brain booze acts on, or what it does chemically. But you would see three Jeffs. There's Jeff, who is . . . which is, you know, enough. He's just an amazing human being. By himself. Then there's booze, which is awful, that's two. And then there's pot, where he becomes what we call the golly green giant. And he's just all funny. He doesn't say very much that's funny. But he's right there funny. I mean you could say the same thing . . . you'd say, for example, shrinks are good people . . . when there's booze, he would come right down on ya. Just come right down, BOOM! And you say the same thing to him on hash, and it just filters in slowly, through the loops, gets in there. Sometimes it happens when he's just himself. And I gotta find ways to change him. . . .

Now I'm double size . . . I'm just about as fat a pig as I've ever gotten. And Monday is the day for cutting out the smoking. That's what he said. We gotta do it for Gilly.

And he goes away to North Carolina overnight Tuesday, and in the middle of the month to Nairobi. And then the money scene is a really bad scene. That's bugging him. And that's always in the back of my mind for quitting. Always. Money. See, he . . . the money scene wouldn't be a hassle. . . . I mean it would be a reality hassle, but it wouldn't be a psychological hassle between the two of us if he felt that I was becoming, what . . . more loving, more whatever the way I used to with Rosenberg. I tried to explain it that Rosenberg was talking about different things. Mucky. It just gets really mucky, this whole therapy thing. I was talking about all kinds of different things with Rosenberg, and I try to explain this to Jeff.

Yea. Jeff asked me, you bad rap me a lot in the *group* and with Becky? And I lied and said, no, and he said, hoping to get off the hook, well, you should because that's where you're supposed to do it. Oh, it's awful, it's just really awful. The way he twists I can't untwist it, but I

56

feel . . . my gut feels the twist even though I sound like an idiot trying to put it to words.

So I do. That's all I've been doing for the last month. Bad rapping him. I think . . . but then . . . I see all the great things there inside him. Maybe part of me is doing that *lovering* bit instead of the bad rap. You explained that to me once, and I'm not sure I understand it. Feeling . . . it . . . the feeling is lovering. Because I love him, and there's no word for it, and it's different from mothering, but it's kind of like that, was what you said. That was really nice when you said that.

And when we were in the museum and I was trying to keep Gilly away so Jeff could enjoy it, I was lovering him. I wasn't mothering him in the museum, I was lovering him. And he can't tell the difference sometimes. Gladstun was wrong. I can't tell the difference too well, either. Because of Gladstun saying that. And because of all the dominant women and how I've . . . and the dominant women in Jeff's life. And, uhh, like Rosenberg said, I had all the wrong role models. Whatever that ugly phrase means. . . . Well, he meant that all the . . . I don't know what he meant. Maybe he was a chauvinist pig. I don't know what he meant. I don't even care. I just know there were a lot of dominant, ugly, fat ladies in my life and a lot of dominant ugly bitches in Jeff's life. And he hates them, and I hate them, too.

I was holding Gilly's hand in the museum, not Jeff's hand. I was giving Jeff freedom. But Jeff felt me holding his hand when I wasn't holding; he felt me mothering when I was lovering. I was saying, here's the museum, groove on it, and I'll hold the world away so you can. And when you're through, tell me, and we'll hold hands.

So it's Jeff's bag. But if I tell him, he'll get a mad on at Becky for another two months. He'll get mad at me and want me to quit. This quitting threat. I know I've got to stop it; it's mucking up therapy. I know and Jeff knows, and you know that I won't . . . can't quit—so please knock it off, Jeff.

57

Doc, maybe I'll just tell Jeff what I learned today, borrow the insights without giving you credit. No footnotes for Becky.

Say, we have thirty seconds left. Would you flex your larynx and tell me something? Can I hurt in intercourse from psychosomatic causes? I probably have a culture growing, which Rosenberg always told me was psychosomatic. He was right. When I would have an orgasm, the culture would go away. But I haven't had one now in quite awhile, and so I've cultures growing. It hurts. In the abdomen, too. I better get it checked. I get so goddamn sick of the psychological shit, I think I'll drum on that for awhile. At least it's physical.

Well time's about up. I think maybe I'll go out and slit a wrist or two.

FOUR

MOOG, THE MAGIC DRAGON

WHY DON'T YOU BUY SOME decent pictures? And a nail. These paintings are terrible. You've lousy taste in art, doc. Sounds like I want to fight, but why should I be a bitch to you? You've said some nice things to me lately, but it's standard procedure for me to fight with the wrong person.

You know, I knew somebody once who'd been in analysis for a really long time. I didn't know her very well. She was a friend's sister. And her cousin told me that before she went into analysis, she was this really nice person. And after her seven or ten year stint, she came out this monstrous bitch. And I wish that would happen to me.

I wish just once whoever it is that makes me angry, I would say, up your ass to that person instead of to somebody else. It's hard to tell the bad guys from the good guys. No . . . I can tell . . . in fact, as I think about it, that's really easy. It's just hard to respond to the bad guys.

Uhm, I'm just in a real bad bag of self-pity, and the only thing that saves me is an old Jewish saw that I heard on a TV program once. And it said, if I'm not sorry for me, who will be? And I guess I'm Jewish enough for that. The *if only* game has stopped. There ain't no more *if onlys*. 'Cause none of them have ever worked. And so there's somebody who is . . . just left with her own reflection to look at. And it's neither comforting, nor nice, nor anything at all. . . . There's nothing to say, doc, nothing.

A friend of Cindy's asked me yesterday, out of the blue, how do you like being a full time housewife? This sort of cracked Cindy up, and there was no answer to the question. As though that were the relevant question. It isn't.

It was interesting what Margaret said about sleeping a lot. I used to do that when I was a freshman in college. If I weren't studying or out on the lawn writing poetry or down at the beach, I was sleeping. It's just really hard to wake up in the mornings. It just is. It feels like it hurts all over, when I try to rap to somebody about it. Otherwise I can do a pretty good number of not feeling at all. That's best achieved when driving. I used to sit in a closet hoping . . . I could, uhh, just become like the schizo ladies in movies and TV shows, where they just sit. You could stick'em with pins, and they didn't move. I thought that would really be nice. You could be alive and dead at the same time. Have your cake and eat it too. I never was very successful at it. I guess I should know that it isn't very pleasant on the funny farm either. I don't know where it is very pleasant.

I guess I grew up thinking that no matter how much the same human beings are, and all the ways that science and even philosophy can analyze them, each one is unique. One really shouldn't think that way. It really . . . you shouldn't . . . I'm not even a good woman's liber. There's no meaningful job that I'm being oppressed from getting. I'd give my eyeteeth if I could go out and earn some bread. I won't do it.

I hate it out there. I hate every contact that I have with it out there. My blinders are coming off. And see, uhm, every little piece of shit that somebody I don't even know pours on me . . . I can't say, because of my condition, you go to hell, you son-of-a-bitch. Like the vet last night. I called, and he said, yea, come down and get him. I'd just been there the night before. They'd taken off his cast, and the poor animal screamed. I thought they were killing him. And they said they were going to keep him to check what was wrong. He said, come down and get Spooky, and so I did. I waited for an hour and a half, until the goddamn

60

guy said, no, we're going to keep him again. Something's wrong with whatever . . . it's nothing . . . not wrong, but he's just sore and can't step on it, we're gonna keep him again. And why didn't I say, you toothless old bastard, why didn't you tell me that on the phone? But I didn't say that. I came home.

And, like Irene screamed that day in the *group*. Rage! With rage! Jeffy understood, and for the first time I understood where he lived all these years. It was Dr. Rosenberg's word, rage. A most apt word. But I never knew what it was. It never existed on my finger tips before. And I guess it was Grace who asked me, does it scare you? God, yes, it does. Because I don't say it to the people who shit on me. I'll call up the manager of Sears and say, God damn you. You took four hundred dollars of our money, and your shitty bed squeaks. Take your goddamn bed and shove it up your ass.

But, you know I've used obscenities so much that they don't even help anymore. There isn't an obscenity that matches what I feel. And if I feel just this little bit of rage . . . good old middle class . . . nothing-having-been-bad-done-to-person, I don't understand why the blacks haven't burned down the fucking country. I'm reading a book now. By a black woman. I don't know why their rage hasn't spilled out before. I don't know why everybody's . . . seems like it's the only thing to explain weird things.

Like that guy who climbed the bell tower at the University of Texas that I read about a long time ago. He just began shooting people. Shot about thirty people. You know, I bet they're very proud of that in Texas. I bet if you'll drive down there, where was it, Austin, some schmuck in a gas station will say, oh yea, that's the bell tower where what's his name shot all those people. They'll really groove on that in Texas. Maybe they're right. Maybe they all know. Maybe they all say, yea. Maybe that's their hero.

There's a man who sits in that White House, who has the power of life and death over all of us. It sounds very dramatic, but it's true. He sends people to dangerous places. After clarifying their identity with a uniform that says I'm here from the man in the White House. And that prick sits in front of TV cameras, while newsmen aim microphones at him. He ain't getting shot at. I'll bet somebody could do an incredible Ph.D. dissertation on him. It's remarkable. Just remarkable.

It's really funny. Helen said to me in the . . . when we were putting on our coats, she said, I know we're not supposed to talk on the elevator, but I've been there, where you are, and I was really with you. And I know it to be true. And I know what Helen says is true, but why doesn't it help? Why won't it help before I climb a bell tower? Like that guy in Texas. I'd do it from the Washington Monument. Greater range. I could shoot more people. Besides they got an elevator that only costs a dime. Do you know—that guy who went out of his gourd in Texas . . . they brought his brain down to a pathology laboratory. As if they could find the rage in his brain by looking at it through a microscope. People are dumb. Well, I'll hang around for Helen's words to help.

What's all that damn hammering down there? You got somebody buried in your floor? You ought to let him out. Shut the hell up down there. Come on, will you? Shut up. . . . You're really a good audience, doc. You always laugh at the dumbest things. You'd be kind of surprised if he would stick his head up through the rug and whisper, hey lady, I wish you wouldn't talk about all that violence.

Poor Gilly. All he sees is this angry Mommy all the time. What a drag it must be. He's got a lot of anger too. Read any good books lately? Uhm, what shall I talk about now? I hate my life, doc. That doesn't mean my circumstances. That means my life. And it's a bad bag, and I'm getting in deeper instead of getting out. And I know all the nice things you said about inner growth, and the life line of attitude change, and all of that, and I believe those. I trust you. I trust the women in the *group*. It's me I don't trust. I don't like relating to Jeff, or to Gil or to Cindy or to anybody. I like just being all by myself . . . I don't know. I know it's really weird that when they're all there I want to get out; like weekends, I want to go places. And when nobody's there, like in the afternoons when Gilly goes to school and everybody's gone, I don't want to go anywhere. I just want to sit. Be all by myself. Not have the noise and the shit from everybody. Not have their pain look at me in the eyes. Not have my responsibility for the parts of their lives that look at me in the eyes. I'm just regressing into being an egocentric little girl. How do you like that? I'm just sick of this whole shit!

You know, the whole world is a Margaret. Is that meaningful? Is that a good metaphor for you? The whole world is a Margaret. And you beat your stupid head against the world because you think, yea, there's something in there, there's something in there. And there's nothing! There's no meaning anywhere.

The most beautiful people I've ever known are dead. So what. So what . . . to anything. Nobody else dropped dead because they did. Nobody else for whom they were responsible suddenly fell apart. Everybody thinks they're so necessary to the function of the life process . . . it's . . . a bunch of crap. It's simply not true. It's . . . even though we all were to believe that it's true.

The old philosophers and priests used to say it; then Hollywood used to say it. Now shrinks say it. Everybody says it. And everybody knows it's a goddamn lie! So what because three hundred thousand people in Peru are dead because of an earthquake. Eighty thousand people die in Vietnam and on the highways, and zillions die of cancer and all the rest, and so what. The planet's gonna die of suffocation from everybody's elbow in everybody else's mouth. So what. You got medicine for inflamation of the elbow? What, elbowitis? Doesn't sound lethal enough. Maybe I should just go back to reading *Little Orphan Annie*.

You're laughing again, doc. I just can't stay serious.

Dieterdoff's fault. I can't ever kill the flip entirely, I guess. Just a little will stay with me forever. Like Rosenberg said, there were probably . . . the greatest jokes were in the ovens as they, pfittt, dropped the little pellets. Somebody made some . . . goddamn Jewish joke! I believe he was right. Those ass-holes were dumb enough to do it. Well . . . I saw a guy on TV, a plastic surgeon who could do all kinds of great things. Do they have ass lifts, do you think? I could sure use one. The flip is growing. Like a mushroom, it's a fungus. Feeds on dead things. That's good. I ought to write that up. Send it in to a great magazine or something. That's really good, I like that.

I'm supposed to be writing stories about Moog, the dragon, for Cindy to illustrate. But I can't seem to do it. They were stories I made up for Gil. And they suddenly stopped because Gil caught on that everytime he heard the word, Moog, he knew something was in store for him. Do I have to go to the doctor tomorrow, Mommy? What's happening? Yea, Moog is an invention of mine. A very distant relative, if at all, of Puff. Because, see. . . . I've heard Puff. . . . I've heard stories that Puff was supposed to be a drug addict. Is that true? But Moog is all together. He's a four year old dragon that lives on a disappearing island, and he has adventures. The island emerges at special times, and Moog does things. Like he goes to the doctor, and like he discovers caves with pirate's treasures. And he has a girl friend, Bubbles. He is terrific. He captures clouds in bottles. Well, that's my son. My son has a marvelous imagination. They're probably killing it at school.

Gilly noticed some clouds once, and he said, wouldn't it be neat if you could go up there with a big jar and get the clouds in the jar and bring it down? And then you could look in the jar and see what was inside the clouds. And wouldn't it be great if you could live up in the clouds and . . . and . . . and have your house up there? And I said, what would hold it up? And he said, I know. We could put a mattress under the house. It was really beautiful. He's got this great, great imagination; he just goes on.

I thought about writing this book called WHAT IF. And use Gilly's what-ifs. And once he starts, he just goes on and on. He once asked Cindy—they had a conversation up in the painting room—and he said, what if you got lonely for your horse? And Cindy said, I'd go home. And Gil said, no, I wouldn't let you 'cause I'd tape up all the doors and windows, and you couldn't get out.

Which was really nice. He's terrific. He's also a pain in the ass sometimes. Gil and Cindy have their own special thing. You know, it's different. Jeff gets really weird about those things. And if anything I say . . . then . . . comes . . . comes the onslaught of defense of the family and the old Jewish thing, bla, bla, bla, bla, bla. But it's true. I mean, all I have to do is look at Gil and ask him. He'd say, yea. Like he said once, after his bath, he whatifed. . . . What if I had two thousand mommies, and three thousand daddies, and five thousand big sisters . . . and twenty thousand Spookies? And I said, Cindy is your cousin, and I don't think he knows what cousin means. So then he changed it to mommies, daddies, and five thousand Cindys. And when she comes home, Gilly hollers, Cindy's home.

I think my sister asked Cindy to come home at the end of the month. She doesn't want to go home. Who'd want to go home to my sister. YEKKK. . . . What a fat bitch she is. She's just a piece of shit. YUCHKK. I hate her.

Good old Izzy, our father. He comes through. He's just simple and straight. And no crap. And you know what I think my sister's doing? She's . . . Cindy and I had this huge, long talk several weeks ago. And I . . . she wrote this big, long tome . . . letter to Cindy. The kind of letters I used to write to my mother, and the kind of letters I used to write to my friends later. Years later. And it threw my mother for a loop, right? So she writes back this big tome, also. Full of the phoniest, crudest crap you could ever imagine. Well, that letter that Sara wrote to Cindy is referred to now by herself and by the other members of the family who were still in Long Island as "The Short Story." Grab that! It sort of sounds weird, but I think Sara's trying to compete with me. Like Jeffy said, when I started to paint, she started to paint. Jeff said a very nice thing. He said, you've never written a letter with shit in it in your life. I used to write pretty long letters, so some of it could seep in. That was nice.

Yea. Cindy thinks the letters are awful. But she's gonna have to go home anyway. Oh, she doesn't want to. She's been witness to so many crazies between Jeff and me that I don't think that she's so particularly thrilled with being in our house either, but she doesn't want to go home, no. She doesn't know what she wants. She's going to be seventeen in two weeks. She's into . . . it's too bad that she's still in high school.

Her biology teacher . . . he's, uhm, twenty-eight or twenty-nine. He's got this beard. He's a really nice fellow, and he really likes her. Except there's this teacher-student thing that's difficult to work out. They have a lot of raps. And he brought her home yesterday. He's been to our house once before just shortly . . . I guess they rap after school and he drives her home. And he's really a nice fellow for her. She's just where everybody always is, who has brains and sensitivity at seventeen. And she's always so surprised to hear other people say the same things that she's feeling. Fortunately I've kept my mouth shut a little bit. But . . . oh, yea. I do slip on occasion and say, Cindy, let me show you the letters I used to write when I was seventeen. Maybe I started a little later than she did. You know—who am I? All that crap.

Yea, she'll go home. What else can she do? I don't know. She has another letter sitting there from Sara today. Cindy misses her horse a lot, and that's the main reason; and the horse was getting fat because nobody rides her. They all take care of her, but nobody but Cindy rides the horse, and she was a little worried about that. And then she has some girl

66

friend who's back there who's a bit older than she is and is already in her first year of college. The kid is writing to her about getting an apartment, and would her folks let Cindy? I mean Cindy's about as naive as what it costs to live by yourself as I would be. As I was in those days. And she knows zilch about those practicalities of life. Maybe she should never know. What good are they anyway? Like checking accounts and shit. I . . . she wants to live off the earth like all the kids want to live off the earth. Well, it's terrific. Marvelous. Uhh, except she doesn't know how to farm.

None of us do. That's . . . that's all lovely. I had those fantasies. So, uhh, you know, you have your babies by natural childbirth. Well, I would have died. And Gil would have died. And even if he had survived, he would have died, and . . . or he would have gone around with a zillion allergies and crosseyed. So you can't live off the earth. The earth ain't no mother. Poor Gil. He has to go once a week for these crappy shots. Ohh boy, is he pissed about that. They're increasing the dose, and it hurts now. And he's thinking, why? Why you sons-of-bitches making me go through all this shit?

So some day, on the moon, he'll be on some moon shrink's couch, and he'll spill it all out. About his rotten, stupid parents. The one . . . the one thing . . . the only thing that a parent, if they're dumb enough to hope at all, is that some day, when their kid is thirty-five, he can come back and say, well, okay, I dig you were a person, and you did do what you thought you had to do. And that's all you can hope for. And you shouldn't even hope for that. Then why should people hope? Except that's the only reason to have kids. To affirm their own being.

Well, what else is new? Enjoy the *Post* today? Von Hoffman's on vacation, so there's nothing new. Art Buchwald stinks. He's really disgusting. I saw him once in Boston. He's just . . . he's not even funny anymore. I mean if you want somebody funny, listen to Richard Nixon. He's really funny. Barbara Howar is good. Judith Martin is good. Maybe the men have shot their wad, and it's the age of women. The women write in a slick way, a slick New York way. It's really funny.

Moog. He keeps invading my head. Damn dragon's too real. The funny thing about Cindy's cartoons is that, see, they are all cross-eyed. They all have these big lashes, and their eyes come together like two converging spot lights. And I asked her—please—when you're thinking up how to draw Moog, not to make him cross-eyed. She knows about Gil. Yea, she knows . . . oh, yea, everybody knows about Gil. And she said, because of Gil? But Moog—M-O-O-G— it's a natural for the eyes to cross. She says, on Moog it looks cute. And when she draws them, they're cute. I guess it caught . . . the feeling for me was that it wasn't so cute.

I never told you about his trauma after his second operation, did I? Well . . . the first time, the eye doctor told me he doesn't bandage the eyes. He said, because I let nature do it, because they'll try to open the eyes and it will hurt, and then they'll just keep their eyes closed until it feels okay, and they will open them. And, ahh, he told me that after. Or some such. Anyway, for the second operation, I knew that was the scene. And finally when they brought Gilly back, he said, Mommy, Mommy, they hurt. And I said, in all good faith, as stupid mothers do, just keep them closed, baby, and they won't hurt. Well, he kept them closed. For three days he kept them closed. I was out of my mind! I called the doctor, and he was most unhelpful via his secretary. He'd never talk to you directly. I called the pediatrician. He didn't really know what to do either. And Jeff came. . . .

And Jeff came home one day, and he said . . . a friend was there, and he said, get out, just get out. Go someplace. Go on. He said he had some things to do. And I left. And what he did was . . . we'd bought a bunch of new toys for Gilly at the hospital, and he . . . he bought him this cannon at the U.N. Building. He'd been into New York

68

City. The city? I guess maybe he had. I don't know. And, uhh, he went into the room, and he shook Gilly awake. And he said, Gil, Michael's stealing your cannon. What? What? What? What? Michael's stealing your cannon. . . . And then Jeff left his room. He went out into the kitchen, and he called somebody up. And he was rapping on the phone, and old Gilly comes waltzing in with all the toys, and the eyes wide open! It was fantastic. It was really beautiful. Would I be lying if I wasn't . . . if I didn't say I wasn't jealous that he did it and I didn't?

I guess the relationship of mother and father to kid is sort of like the wife takes a jar of pickles and bangs at it with a knife, you know, for five minutes and can't open it. It takes the husband . . .he goes like . . . a simple, easy twist, right? That's it. . . . So why the hell am I crying? That guy in the pharmacy always says my eyes and nose are red. Come to think of it, that guy in the pharmacy shouldn't talk about anybody else's nose. Then again, doc, maybe because of a nose like his—he feels it gives him a right.

FIVE

A WALL COMES TUMBLING DOWN

I HAVE A ZILLION THINGS TO TALK about today. I'm feeling a lot less depressed, but I'm still awful nervous, and I'm not sure why. Tuesday, you said some really nice things to me . . . about me in the *group* and . . . and that was . . . really neat. It was an incredible session. I felt so happy about Margaret. It was just . . . it was just really neat. You said the word *nidus,* and I didn't know what that meant, but you used another word later, that I got into the middle of the storm. And you explained to Irene for me that I wasn't mad at her, even though I start to shake when I get talking that way. That I envy her in a way. And, uhm . . . I don't know. I just really like that. It felt so real . . . your presence on my side. Didn't you think that was nice?

Okay, well . . . don't answer then. It happened to be nice. Yea. I mean I happen to . . . I mean I just liked it. I liked the whole session. I liked you. And I felt jolly for the whole rest of the day. Uhm, the angers are still there. Lots of angers. They seem to be not erupting as much, but they still tend to erupt.

I'm learning to pinpoint the angers, especially when they concern the outside world. That's something I've never done before. And the whole thing about anger is kind of new because, uhm . . . I'm . . . I think it's true that in the *group* the word hostility has never been used. And what I'm . . . what I've been experiencing then, in the muddy waters, is awful anger.

It's such a different kind of thing from the old days

71

when I called all this shit hostility. It's just such a different bit of business. Like hostiles always belong to the person who's feeling them. And it's always some icky thing in them that's causing it. Things that are impossible for me to nail down. That's how it always struck me, and you know, it was legitimate at the time. Now the anger is something else. There's an object. Not always necessarily out there. It can be me. But there's an object. Feeling anger is not like this stew, like this soup. It's . . . it's not totally clear to me . . . because it's very new and different but . . . well, anyway. It's different and I like it. I mean I don't like to feel the anger, but . . . I'm. . . . Aah, shit, I never do know what's gonna happen in this room. I'm getting balled up here.

There. It's happened again. I'm just caught by surprise right now. That I suddenly felt like a blithering idiot. I had it straight in my head, and whap, like a blithering idiot's talking. So then folks, she said to herself, take it again from the angers. What about the angers, Pam? Oh, about the angers . . . well, it's this way, doc. . . .

You see what's happened with the angers . . . well, let me back up a minute. Often I have said, other people have said, too, in the *group,* I don't understand what is going on with myself. Whatever. And, uhm . . . Margaret . . . I remember saying to her, do you have to understand? Is that important to you? Because she said the need to understand was a thing for her. And it always has been important to me to be able to articulate. Often I think that articulation was just . . . uhm . . . not necessarily also understanding. But it passed for that on occasion. The place where I am and have been for the last couple of weeks is not at all amenable to understanding on my part. Or articulation. And it's, uhm . . . it . . . it's just. . . . It just is! I don't really want to use the two fancy words that pop into my head like existential and phenomenology. It just is!

Like the anger—is. The muddy waters—are. And the fact that Tuesday I was coming out of it before I got to

72

the *group*—just was. Part of that was having an orgasm for the first time in a hell of a long time. I tend to be really absolute about that. If it . . . I . . . uhm . . . I think . . . on all these kind of things, if it's negative, it's gonna be negative forever.

And it always reminds me of years ago, when I lived with the Cohens when I was going to college. I was a mother's helper and maid for my room and board. Anyway, Mimi had a breast removed. It was a rough deal. And, uhm . . . oh, some relative of hers was giving a lot of shit to Rubin about it—that Mirium's gonna be really depressed, bla—bla, bla—bla, bla—bla. And Rubin said, nyeech, one good fuck and she'll feel fine. And you know, it's terrific. Because, uhm . . . good sex is a really important thing.

It's not the whole story, but it's a big part of it. And as I was driving down here today, I was thinking . . . uhm . . . a lot of things . . . or a number of things about that. One is that Jeff . . . what I called the internist for was to change Jeff's tranquilizer from that awful pill. I talked to him and told him that Jeff didn't like what it did as a tranquilizer, and besides, that it seemed to be having the . . . uhh, uhh, uhh . . . effect of impeding Jeff's maintaining an erection. He said, God, if that keeps on, you must call me! So he prescribed a different pill, and that's fine. The new one doesn't do that thing to him.

And I thought that whatever hassles that Jeff and I have sexually, difficulties or whatever, that eighty-five percent of it is me, ten percent is him, and five percent of it is the shit of the world that gets at you during the day to exhaust you and make you angry and do all the things that muck you up. But the big . . . that's about as straight as I can make it with numbers. And it's all tied up with the smoking and the eating and the whole . . . all of it.

I'm about . . . except for the time I was pregnant, I'm as fat as I've ever been in my whole life. Ever. I've never been here before. And trying to quit smoking was, you know, really impossible. I've cut down a lot, though I've broken some of the rules and smoked in the house, probably because Jeff does that. We confine it to the kitchen mostly, so that there's not smoke all over the house. That's because of Gil. But I've increased it some in an effort to keep me from eating. Today I've done pretty well. Yet, I'm scared on two counts. I'm scared that I'm not gonna lose weight, and I'm scared that I am. And, uhm . . . that's as far as I've gotten with it. I still don't know why I'm so scared to lose weight. It wasn't scarey, I don't . . . unless I blocked it all. In Boston, three years ago when I really lost a lot of weight, went to about 123, which is about 30 pounds under what I'm now, and I don't remember it being scarey back then.

Maybe it was. Maybe it was scarey with my sexual fantasies about Chuck. I don't know. Let me tell you more about Chuck. I can't remember what I've told you and what I haven't, so I might repeat. You told me it's okay to . . . repeat. I really dug him. I still do. There was no action, except in, you know, dancing close together and that kind of shit. Or wandering around talking while we watched the kids in the apartment building. Yea, I liked him a lot. And he liked—I'm gonna say us—because he liked both of us very much. He was really sad when we left Boston. He was really crushed that I was so excited to be leaving. I could see it on his face. It was wild.

And I can hear it when he calls once a year, or however often he calls. I told you it's never Lana or Lillian, Tim's wife, who calls. It's always Chuck and Tim. Have I talked to you about Tim? I was always closer to both of them than to the women. I really dug both of them. I didn't have any sexual thing for Tim. I used to like to talk religion with him 'cause he'd been at a seminary. He was a Catholic, and it was fun. And Chuck was impossible in politics. He was a conservative, and anti-communist and that kind of shit. Boy, doc, did I have it bad for Chuck. Really wanted . . . uhm, but never got into his pants. Part of it was all the problems Jeffy and I were having. What can I say? I don't know what to say. Makes me sad. I don't know why.

Maybe it's the thought of good times lost. I'm not sure. I'm not sure whether I mean the recall of past friendships or that we're so far apart. And by we, I mean all of us, because they were fun and good friends. Uh . . . or the . . . fantasy . . . the feeling, fantasy . . . the . . . all of it together. Whether that's what makes me sad or the non-fulfillment of any of it.

But thinking about it . . . it's sad. To have experienced such deep involvement, that now transcends vast geographic boundaries. It exists as a memory now. On only a handful of moments do such relationships occur. It's a sad thing. Maybe that's what's making me sad . . . is that they are far away. And there hasn't been anything like that since we left there. And that's . . . that's almost three years. Three years? It can't be. Over three years. Wow. Like I said. I think I said that after we left Boston to go back to New York was when the era of Chuck closed. And now we're in Washington, and it's still closed.

Help me with the fat, doc. I know you said when I wanted to lose it, I would. Well, I want the thin. Lean and trim and . . . sexual. But that's something which I'm afraid of. I am. I associate with an image of woman's lib. I'm afraid to be a liber. Afraid. See there's always, uhm . . . there's always the hang-up. Now these are . . . this is an area where it's really, where it's . . . just so difficult to separate me from Jeff. Even in the choice of words, I have a really hard time telling him from me. So to separate feelings is even worse. Where my feelings are and where his are. . . .

But what I'm afraid of is wanting . . . uhm . . . wanting sex . . . sexual expression on my terms. Now, that phrase is his. It's a phrase I hate. Because . . . goddamn it, I want it on my terms. I . . . see . . . what feels to me like being free, feels to him like, *always on your terms,* said through the teeth. Am I getting through? You sneezed. Bless you. The sneeze sounded sarcastic. Maybe not. See how messed up . . . mixed into one I get when I define our sexual . . . feelings? Needs? Well, uhm . . . what can I say? The moments I feel the freest, when I'm really digging sex, those are the moments I get it thrown back in my face that I'm . . . uhm . . . what? I don't know the words he uses. Pushy. Trying to dominate. Trying to domineer. Trying to call the shots. Trying to be boss of the show. That's. . . . I'm . . . that's not what he's ever said, but. . . . All those things. And it's one of those situations where, uhh, you stick in, and you think you're being straight, and you get shit thrown in your face. If I'm on top, I should be on the bottom. Get what I mean?

And it confuses the hell out of me. Scares the hell out of me. Turns me off, and I say, screw it, I don't want to go there. So I get fat, so I don't have to go there.

Now, I don't mean Jeff's physically cruel—no! I mean just that it is about as cruel to me as you can get. It's like saying to somebody, hey, I like you. And then they say, go to hell. Maybe . . . see . . . I don't know. I don't know what's real in all of this. I don't know . . . whether what I say is my feeling free, is my feeling free, or whether it really is trying to call the shots or trying to put him down. I don't know. I just don't know. I can just tell you how I respond.

Maybe . . . maybe it comes out h . . . host . . . to use the old word, hostile. Maybe I do come on like a hostile bitch. Dominating. I don't know, I don't. I don't know. I can't even give you a for instance. And I don't feel I'm betraying Jeff. That's not it. No. I'm just blocking it really fast. So I can't feel it in my brain. I have a feeling I'm . . . I'm lying about this freedom stuff. 'Cause, see, I'm saying it through my teeth. And, uhm . . . I'm getting a clue from that, that goddamn it, I am coming on like a ton of bricks. I'm coming with a knife. Not love.

That's what he feels. That there isn't any giving, just taking. Getting. Not really taking—getting! Though he's never used that word. See, in those moments that . . . to change the verbs, maybe that . . . those moments, I don't want to get laid, I want to fuck! And if you just heard the anger come out in that, maybe it all goes back to the old P.E. Complex that the ladies didn't know what I was talking about. How can those ladies not know about *penis envy.* Maybe it is just all that old shit. I don't know.

That's about as close as I can come, doc. . . . That wasn't quite the right word to use. It's C-O-M-E, doc. How is the other spelled? I never saw it spelled. I guess it depends on which bathroom you walk into. But I've never seen it. Is it C-U-M? Oh, yea? It never occurred to me.

That P.E. Complex. It's a curious thing. You accused me of swiping it from Rosenberg or Kaplin when I said it in the *group.* But I didn't. I don't know where that came from. Probably from *Psych* 1-0-1. I don't think, I mean, all . . . I don't think any shrink ever laid that on me. I think it was just talk among people. You know what happens when you take *Psych* 1-0-1. You're suddenly a shrink, right? And I was still a senior in high school when I took it. I think it must go back to there because I don't remember Rosenberg or Kaplin or even my prick shrink, Olson, ever giving me that stuff. None of them ever gave me Freudian stuff. I mean labels. I used to beg for labels.

That's what made me laugh when you gave Maxine that terrific label. That's a rotten son-of-a-bitching label. What you called her. Passive-aggressive. One psychology teacher once laid that label on me, and it was awful. I hated it. Passive-aggressive. Yuchh. What is that anyway? I don't know what that is. It was just a label that seemed to fit how I felt when I was a little girl, that's all.

It was just a crying shame I didn't have a cock. The same feeling isn't there for balls. It was just so much easier to pee with one. That was it. And I've always felt that way. I still do. It's just you know, so much easier for, say . . . you go to the woods, and Gil has to pee, so he goes by a bush and he pees. And if you're a girl who has to pee, she has to go behind a bush so she can take off all her panties and her socks and spread her legs so she doesn't

77

get all wet, and the whole thing. It's just . . . I heard one little girl, a neighbor, who's five years old, and she said, it's so much easier for little boys. They just take it out and squirt. And that's what it is. I mean that's what I felt. As a plumbing fixture, the vagina is second best to the penis. Oh, well, never mind.

You get a whole bath in here. I get a whole bath. One gets wet in here, remember that? How I used to sweat like crazy when I first started to use the couch. It flooded out . . . like now. Got a towel?

Grace's always told me to ask you to show me the birthday . . . the uhm, Christmas card she made for you. Some rotten joke about the Virgin. She's always telling me rotten jokes about the Virgin Mary, which I find sort of interesting. I don't know if she tells the other ladies her rotten jokes about the Virgin. I know she believes in the Virgin, whatever that means. Maybe she thinks I'll understand rotten jokes about the Virgin. Maybe remem . . . maybe she knows that my grandmother used to tell me the same rotten jokes when I was a little girl.

Well, I feel I haven't gotten anywhere at all today. I feel sort of like Maxine. That everything's coming apart at the seams. I wonder if I have to torture myself in here and feel shitty in order to feel I'm getting somewhere. No, that's not true, doc. I suddenly feel shitty, and that's why I think I'm not getting anywhere. You dig that? First the shit feeling, then not getting anywhere in that order.

How come you walked out last week . . . you left a patient sitting in here and came out into the waiting room to see if I was all right. Were you worried about me? That was really nice. I didn't expect that at all. That was really nice.

I haven't written about Moog yet, except in my head. And I prepared a canvas four days ago, and I haven't painted. I'm really tired. I wish I could explain tired. I mean describe the tired to you. I don't know how to do it. It's a let-me-alone-tired.

78

What happens in that *group*, though, is just unbelievable. It was so wild when Helen said, I felt like you had a rope out there for Margaret. And that's exactly how I experienced it. A rope. And the woman grabbed it! It's just really nice. You helped her to get into things again. Very subtly. But you did, and she knew it and she grabbed on. Later, after the *group*, out in the hallway . . . you must really get a bigger room or a bigger building or something. It's getting really crowded, with all these winter coats and everybody sticking their elbows in everybody's eyes. And Helen said to me, she said, you're such a perceptive person or woman. I don't know which she said. And I said, uhm, I happen to believe that's true, but it's difficult to say yes, like the lady in the commercial, yes, that's true. I said, yea, but I can't do it on me. And Grace said her line that she's laid on me before, like, if you're so smart, how come you're here? And we laughed a little bit about that. And I walked out the front door of the building with Margaret and Maxine, and I said, good-bye, to both of them. And then I turned around and yelled, really loud, good-bye Margaret.

It was just really nice. Good old Margaret. I've learned more from Margaret, reacting with Margaret, than from anybody else. It's wild. Of all people. How can a person learn from a wall? Oh, maybe she ain't such a wall. At least a brick was taken down. You could see it falling. It must have blown her mind. For some reason, I'm . . . I guess . . . I don't know why. For all the anger that her wall produced in me, underneath I've always liked her wall better than Maxine's. I don't have any real interest in breaking through Maxine's wall. I don't even know if it's right to call that a wall. I don't know where the hell she is. She's just hardly even there. She's like the ladies I used to watch in Saks. You know Saks? It's a department store more like Garfinckels, or Lord & Taylor, than like Woodies or Hecht. And it's across the street from C.C.N.Y. or down in the village from C.C.N.Y. Always very simply dressed. Not with globs of jewels and shit and minks, just very simply dressed. A kind of quiet, uhh, uhm . . . what? . . . confidence. I don't know if it was true or not. I just used to watch them. Look at them. A kind of class.

And when Maxine's sitting down, she looks that way. I haven't watched her walk or move. She's short. She's even shorter than I am. She doesn't look that way when she sits down. And she says such awful shit. God, she says terrible shit. Just dribbles out of her mouth. Pellet after pellet. She doesn't even know it. Like when we introduced ourselves to the new lady that joined the *group,* and she said, I ping when I should pong. Oh, God it was so awful. She's . . . she's just laughable, she's just blah.

Maybe because I feel she's a whole different generation. Maxine. If you . . . she just lives someplace I don't want to live. Even just from her daily life. And her religion. And all that good and evil and all that garbage. Margaret's good and evil is something different. That's not superficial stuff. She's metaphysically evil. That's how she thinks of herself. And that's interesting. Yea, I like Margaret. I realized that after, uhh . . . when was it . . . uhm . . . last week whenever it was when you said she should be grateful that we were still at her, because it's hard to beat your head against a wall. And I thought about that, and I thought there's something underneath it. Maybe I said it Tuesday, I don't remember. There was something about her that didn't show in the *group,* until this Tuesday, but outside that room, when we walked out the door, and she smiled, then it was a different smile. And I guess I never thought about it. I just felt it. There was something there.

I liked her the first time that I met her, when she rejoined the *group.* What was the story? Something about she had to quit the *group* for a while because her husband had to move his work to California for some months? I liked her that first day. Back then I had a totally different impression. I thought she was really bright, and really with it, and was like a Grace. Well, you know. There it goes. So much for my first impression. Uhm, not to say that I don't think

80

she's bright. But she's certainly not like Grace. Uhm, yea, I like her. I like Helen. I like Grace, although something else is happening with me about Grace. She's beginning to bug me. I'm scared of her. I realize now I am. You know I've never been blasted by any of those people in *there*. Nobody's ever blasted me. And, uhm . . . I don't think I'm too eager to have it happen.

Irene is something else. I'm constantly changing about her. The week she walked in looking like somebody's old cameo, uhm . . . I don't know. I have a small sculpture at home. It's just of the torso; has no head or arms or legs. And the terrible thing is, when I was pregnant, the bigger I got, the skinnier this thing got. And literally, it was the only visual—I don't know if it was a hallucination or what —the only visual kind of thing that I'd ever experienced since. And ever since. And this thing just kept getting smaller and smaller. It's just really weird. And that seems to be happening with me with Irene. The fatter I get, the skinnier she seems to be. Except I'm not pregnant now. That's why I had hoped that Jackie would stay in the *group*. Because she was another fatty. At least there would be two of us. There's just one of me now.

Gilly and I were out shopping the other day, and we saw this gigantic lady. Just gigantic. She took up three quarters of the sidewalk. And he said to me, hey Mommy, you know those women? Oh, he's terrific. Oh, that's awful. Oh, he's neat. I really roared, and I was embarrassed lest she heard me laugh. Isn't that funny, doc? Doc? You awake? Oh, you bastard.

Six

TO CEASE TO BE

I'LL TRADE YOU, DOC. You can view my painting if
you'll give me a prescription for some tranquilizers. Last
session I told you I prepared a canvas. Well, I got something
on it now, and here it is. Do you like my painting? What
about the tranquilizers? Huh? Listen, I gotta have something
so I can quit making my family miserable. If you'll order
me just three or four, that's terrific. I don't need anymore
than that. But something. I can't keep dumping on my
family. I'm rotten to Gil, rotten to Cindy. Fortunately, Jeff's
not here this week or I'd be rotten to him. I was rotten to
him last week. I've taken maybe two of Jeff's tranquilizers,
and they help. I mean, it doesn't . . . I don't want anything
that gives me a big high, or knocks me out or sends me up
the wall. But the . . . something to just cool the angers for
awhile. Something that takes the look of garbage off my face.

And . . . you know, the painting and the writing Moog
stories and all that shit that's supposed to make me feel
nice. Well it doesn't. I did this canvas and I still feel shit.
If I'm gonna stick around, I might as well stick around
with a less ugly look. If I stick around.

That's only in reference to my fantasies. I mean the if.
If I . . . uhm . . . stay in this place. I fantasize driving in
the goddamn woods. I don't fantasize popping pills until
I'm dead. That's the chicken's way out.

I fantasize driving in the woods. Into the woods! I fantasize going over the beltway. Off the goddamn beltway. I
hesitate to tell you . . . anybody about those fantasies

'cause most people take it as a crock of shit. I think about it all the time. There ain't no hope, doc.

You know, my bright brain says, boy, lady, you're in the same place as a zillion other people. You think you're a big zero. And they think they're a big zero. And you think your problems are unique and extraordinary and painful and so do they. And so what! That's why it has been really difficult for me lately in that *group*. Aside from the fact that there are two new people that knew what I said. Why did you have to put two more ladies in the *group*, doc? I mean who in the goddamn *group* wants to know I fantasize going over the beltway? Nobody. Who cares? And I don't care if they fantasize it either. More people probably ought to kill themselves. They got the right.

So you just finally . . . there isn't more to say. And it's just a big silence. And the silence . . . whether I rap, whether I bitch, whether I scream and holler at home, whether I walk around with my face with garbage on it, it bugs people! It drives them up the wall! 'Cause they're trying to do their own survival. You dig it?

I'm mucking up my little boy's life. Jeff and Cindy and anybody else I know can survive with or without me. With my shit or without my shit.

But it's not fair to Gil who's only five, who can't defend himself against this gross bitch. And I take a lot out on him. And he's got his own troubles. Poor kid can't even breathe half the time. And I'm not at all sure that it's all allergy or all bronchial infection. I'm not at all sure that it's not just a big response to me and my constant angers, my constant irritations, my constant ugliness. I scream at him all the time. I tell him, don't bug me. Don't bother me. Go play by yourself. And I scream at him. I don't just say it, I don't just say, look, I'm tired. Look, I'm angry now. I scream at him, get outta here, you fucking kid.

It's really terrific. And it doesn't even work if I try not to do that. It's just . . . it's just shit oozing out of me. And there ain't nowhere to go. Except off the beltway. Wham,

84

into the woods. I just. . . . I've lost all control, doc. I hate getting up in the morning. I hate it. I'd give anything never to wake up again. I gotta get out of here.

I gotta stop ruining Gil. Look, if I don't call you tomorrow morning, fill my time slot with another nut. I'm tired of crying all the time. I'm tired of all the sads. I'm going . . . into the woods . . . maybe . . . end the shit on Gil.

SEVEN

FLOWERS AND FUNERALS

MY PAINTING . . . RIGHT WHERE I LEFT it last week. You know, two weeks ago you left a patient and came into the waiting room to see if I was okay. Remember? And last week, when I left the office to go over the beltway, you just sat in your goddamn chair. I walked out after only five minutes on my way to die. And you didn't even come out to check on me. Shit on you, too. Wasted fifty bucks, and you didn't even come out. Screw you. I mean it. I really needed you, and I like you a lot. What would you have done with my painting if I'd have gone over the beltway? Yea, was I low last week. Really low. I still am, but not as bad. I still worry and wonder about the damage I'm doing to Gil. And, uhm . . . decided . . . I felt he needed me more than he didn't. So I'm here. Welcome me back, doc.

You know, we got rid of Spooky. God damn dog. Stupid vet. He fixed the break in his leg, but . . . he took the cast off. This stupid dog screamed. They kept him for three stupid days. They found he had a deformed hip, and they said, the hell with it. Take him to the shelter. And Jeff said, well, okay, I'll do it. Well, poor Jeffy couldn't do it, right? He was up all night with some idiots about finalizing some contract. So I did it. Fortunately Cindy came with me. Some dumb lady at the shelter made some crack, and I said, here . . . you know . . . here's Spooky . . . and I cried. So what did Jeff and Cindy and Gil do? They said, get another puppy, right? And I said, are you sure you want another puppy?

87

See, I made the mistake. I should have said, no. Goddamn it. I don't want another ass-hole dog around here whose shit I have to clean up. All of them say, oh, terrific. Let's have this swell dog that will live up to the Beware-of-Beast sign. And I wanted to yell, but you guys don't clean up his shit. You don't whack him with a newspaper. You don't do anything but say, gee, we got a neat dog here. So we bought a dog.

A black german shepherd who's gonna grow up to be an elephant. His father weighed 140 pounds. Exactly what we need. He's seven weeks old, and he shits and pisses all over. You stick his nose in it, and he thinks it's terrific. He eats it. And every morning I have to wake up and wash the kitchen floor, before I even, you know, blow my nose. It's funny, and it's not funny. It sets me to screaming before anybody else even wakes up.

And Jeff talks about the tension in the household. Why is there so much tension in the household? How come you've been going to therapy for a zillion months and you're getting worse? I don't know why he asks why, when he is a big part of the answer to his own question. Now he's in Peru. So he's in Peru, and he goes to South America. There isn't any contact till he comes home. I don't know what's happening there. Whether it's good. Whether it's miserable. Whether it's awful. He really didn't want to go. I've never seen him before . . . act the way he did . . . like he did before leaving on this trip. He put off packing until half an hour before. He was exhausted and tired and had a few drinks. God, he was just a mess. He hates going on these trips. That's true. But I'd never seen him quite this way. It really scared me.

I finally said, they'll never kidnap you there. They couldn't stand you for five minutes. They'd beg the people to take you back. And now he's coming home Saturday, and here I am. Gil has been home two days with a goddamn 'nother infection. The doctors tell me, wait. Wait. We'll finish the second bottle of allergy shit, and you'll see some effects.

88

Terrific. I don't believe it. I think it's just a crock. They're just pouring crap into the kid's body. For two days he did nothing but cough and throw up. And my response, good old mother that I am, is not comfort. It's anger. The goddamn rotten generation of the 1950's. I do worse things than our parents did to us. God, is it the nature of it?

For your information, I didn't paint the painting the way you're looking at it. I set it that way last week because it looks like octipi and jelly fish and icky mummies. You know, the Smithsonian has some great mummies. All these ugly bodies with their hair and their teeth. Nancy and I took our kids to the museum. She said, oooh, I hope the children don't have nightmares. I said, keep your mouth shut, and they won't. And I got down on all fours, and I talked to the kids about these bodies. These mummies.

And Gil says, it's kind of icky. And I said, it's not icky. They used to be people. They used to be alive and laughing. The kids were just wide-eyed. They couldn't believe it, They loved it, and they were like hypnotized. Not scared at all. It's interesting. They all thought it was terrific. They only have nightmares when their mother says, that causes you nightmares. Well, that's the same thing I'm doing with my kid. In slightly different ways I do the same equally stupid and horrible things to Gilly. There is no doubt that I do. Jeff tells me I do. It's true. I can't say it all in only fifty minutes with you each week. I could never say it in the two hours with *ladies* each week.

I told Gilly I was a rotten mother. That I was sorry I was rotten. He says, you're not a rotten mother. You're a lovely mother. Stupid kid. Doesn't know any better. He will.

The computer room is finished at Jeff's place downtown. It's been running. Getting a lot of play because everybody's been waiting its completion. And they hung two of my paintings in there. You know, the one you called the sperm painting. With all the flagella. You got a dirty mind, doc. Then another one you didn't see. One Jeffy liked a lot that was in his office. They hung it up in there. He tells me all these things. Everybody tells me they're wild and terrific and great. And you see it when you walk in, bla-bla-bla. . . . Goddamn thing was warped when I saw it, when I took Gil to their Christmas Party. I told Jeff to bring it home. I said, you're not gonna hang that up there. It's all warped. The nails are coming out of the frame. He said, well, I'll have somebody fix it up.

But . . . he . . . you know what bugs me, why I never wanted to give him any of the paintings to hang down there? 'Cause he doesn't do it on my terms. It's my goddamn painting. I painted the damn thing. If somebody wants to see blue noses in there and three eagles flying, that's terrific. But that's their bag, not mine. But he tells everybody, Pam calls it *Blaw-blaw,* and she painted it for the conference room. Well, in a certain sense that is true. I mean, I damn well may title the painting, but he knows absolutely that I didn't do it for the conference room. I did it for me, and I gave it to Jeff.

But . . . see, the point is . . . what he sees in it, he sees in it. It wasn't mine. And he would never understand in a million years if I told him that. So the painting doesn't give me much of a thrill. He's always done that. One time some old drunk that used to live in our apartment in Boston, his wife was out of town, and he came in. There's a painting there that I call my birth painting because that was how Rosenberg interpreted it. And it really hit me . . . and I rather liked it. It was the first thing I ever . . . I did that I liked . . . that was a real painting. Not just crapping around. Uhh, after . . . I started painting after Gilly was born. And, uhm, this guy was so smashed, he said, look at that. I see Mao Tse-tung in there. He was going on and on, and it really gave him a thrill. And I said, that's nice. You know, I didn't care who he saw in there; what he saw in it. And it didn't affect how I felt about it. It was terrific. That's okay.

But he didn't say, you painted Mao Tse-tung. Look, everybody, Pam painted Mao Tse-tung. Why does Jeff do that? You know, for me that's a put down, and he wouldn't understand that either. He's putting me down . . . by doing that. By making it something other than what I say it is. So the *I* is gone! Boom! Out! The *me* ain't when Jeff gets hold.

I just . . . I don't know . . . I guess I disappoint so many people. . . . Well, they disappoint me. Cindy disappoints me. We had a long talk a couple of weeks ago. Jeff was getting kind of bugged again with her and didn't think she . . . you know . . . he felt she wasn't helping. So I said, all right. Let's. . . . I'm not too good at making rules. You do the dinner dishes and vacuum a couple of times a week, and we'll let it go at that, and anytime you baby-sit for us, I'll pay you. I'd already done that from the beginning. I told her, I'll pay you a quarter an hour, so that neither of us feels used or cheated. Well, goddamn it, the shit doesn't even do it. Or if she does, she does it half-ass. You know, minimum. Okay. Seventeen years old. I was the same way. But it drives me up the wall, I can't say anything. I try and say it. I try to say it straight to her—you do the minimum.

I don't know . . . out of the household . . . you know, there are fantastic egos. Maybe my own. I don't know. I don't know which end is up or who's where. It's like being caught in the middle of an old Abbott and Costello thing. Who's on first?

This . . . this couple that we met in Czechoslovakia, who . . . were over there for . . . they live in Bethesda. They came back. They sent us a Christmas card and said to get in touch with them. I finally called. I was really scared. I'm still scared to call people.

The *Art Patch* is having a sculpture thing. They have them in the mornings when I can't go, and they said they were going to try an evening class, Tuesday. Well, I was really excited about that. I mentioned it to Jeff. I said, before that, I said, the *Art Patch* is gonna have a sculpture thing on Tuesday. You know what his response was? The bastard told me, you've gotta get *our* thing in for the Spanish class. You know, the Spanish class. Because I gotta help him with the Spanish so that he can impress people in Ayacucho, so that he can make money, so that I can come to the shrink.

I was gonna go Tuesday, but I didn't go. Not to learn how to make pots. I was gonna go . . . maybe there was somebody there who could be a friend. It's . . . whatever that means anymore. I don't even know. All I know is I miss Jeff a lot. On the other hand, it's nice not to have to get his coffee and clean the shit up from the dog at the same time in the morning. Maybe I'm just too wrapped up in my own self. Maybe I ought to just go out and dig. . . . Clean up garbage for poor families or something. I want to go into the *group* and scream my bloody head off. Well, I can't.

It's just so weird. I remember when my friend, from New York, was out here in that crazy week in May, and I said, all I got are these stupid paintings. And she looked at me like I was from outer space—all you got are your stupid paintings? She said, if I could just do one of those stupid paintings. And so I looked at me . . . you know . . . thinking about times when people say, you can really express yourself. So what! I said, yea, relatively speaking I guess it's better than . . . than not being able to paint at all.

You know there is an incredible thing; I don't know if you ever watch documentaries. But they had a thing on television . . . there's one about . . . of these . . . on Carmelite orders. These ladies who go in, and that's the end. Don't mess with the world, ever again. They marry their Jesus Christ, and that's it, and they're really happy. Maybe they're insane. Who knows? Maybe we're insane. But they sure got some secrets that nobody else has. I told you Dieterdoff once said to me if I ever saw the *Vatican,* I would be instantly converted. Dieterdoff was a very sensitive guy. Some teachers you just never forget.

Oh, funny thing. Along those same lines. Not really

changing the subject. When I was in the pharmacy with Gil, getting his medicine, and he likes these kind of post cards that . . . uhm . . . shimmer, sort of. And he likes . . . he digs those, and lately whenever I'm there to buy something, I ask him if he's got the money for it. He's got to pay me out of his pennies. We pay him to feed the dog and clean up the den. And he said, yea. And I said, okay, pick one out. And they had the Washington Monument and all these. So he picked one out, and I didn't notice it. I just paid for it with everything else. And later when we got home, I saw it on the dining room table. You know what he picked out? He picked out *The Last Supper.*

It was fantastic. My mouth fell open. I really am surrounded by Catholics. I said, how come you picked this card? He said, well, look at the pretty colors the people are wearing and the pretty colors in the ceiling and stuff. And I said, you know it's a reproduction of a painting that's in Italy, and it's called *The Last Supper.* He knew I thought it was weird. I couldn't hold that back. He said, well, it's really pretty, don't you think? And I said, yea, it's really pretty.

I remember once in art history class, there was a blow-up: a slide blow-up of Christ from *The Last Supper.* Leonardo's *Last Supper.* It was very moving. And Mirium Cohen . . . you know, the family I lived with at school . . . it was only years later that she told me . . . you know . . . I used to have . . . I took so many art history courses . . . I used to cut out stuff from *Time* and shit and hang it up on the wall. And they were all crucifixions or the pieta or the taking Christ down from the cross and all this shit. Because I figured then . . . I . . . I . . . never painted it. I did take that one drawing course . . . but I figured the only subject worthwhile painting was the crucifixion. Even though most of the time it's done badly, there are a few good ones. So my kid brings home *The Last Supper.* Jeff will throw up when he sees it. He's never heard Gil go into his number, God is great, God is good, 'cause they do that shit at school.

So what have you got to say, doc? I wish I could get my angries straightened out. I mean—at whom. Yea. Like nobody ever knows which way I will explode. Least of all, me. Like right now I hate the people who are painting your goddamn hallway because I can't stand the smell of paint. The artist said. So I might explode at Gil, throwing anger onto him. He doesn't recoil. He just gets his own damn angries. He says, oh, fuck it! That's what the kid says. He slams doors, just like I do. He's . . . he . . . just . . . it's just me there.

He does. He says, oh, fuck it. I can't call the kids. I'm sad! I'm miserable! Don't talk at me. Don't tell me it's time to go to sleep. He just screams it at me. He screams like I do. He mimics. It is not that he's consciously mimicking. You know how they . . . they always come back at you with your own words. Well, he's coming back at me with the anger. I mean, over a year ago, this was an enormously angry little boy when we moved to Washington. And I worked hard so that he wouldn't just, uhm . . . display it all over the world. He lived in New York and loved it. Then Boston. Then back to New York. Now Washington. Move. The word move sets him off. He's angry! He's very sad. The kid doesn't lie. He just says it. When somebody's bugging you, you say, oh, fuck you! Well, that's what he says. And fortunately he has that beautiful language from his mother.

And what do I say? I say it back. I say, oh, shut up. Or I calm down and I say . . . I don't know what I say. Sometimes I try to be rational. He knows I love him. But so what. Is that gonna help him? I wish I could stop crying. It messes up my thinking. Is it? Is that gonna help him? Maybe it will. My mother never screamed at me, and I never thought that she loved me. I hope he knows I love him.

He asked me the other day. . . . You know he hollers

94

into the room. It's a habit in our awful household. He says, what would you do if somebody was trying to kill me? I said, I'd do everything to stop them, including killing them. And he knows I don't like killing. I said, I'd do everything including stepping in front of him and taking the bullet myself. He said what would daddy do? I said, he'd do the same thing. He would hit him on the head, or shoot him or step in front or do whatever he could. And Gil said, why would you do that? And I said, why do you think? He said, to save me 'cause you love me. And I said, that's right. And we let it go at that.

He's always asking things like that. He asked me once, what would you do if I died? I said, I don't want to talk about awful things like that. He said, what would you do? I said, I'd feel really sad. He said, wouldn't you bring flowers to my funeral? And it cracked me up, and I said, yea, I'd bring flowers. And he said, that's nice, you have to bring flowers to show you care. Dumb kid. He's really bright.

What difference does it make if I love him? I'm still putting shit on his head. I know people put shit on the heads of those we love most. I know. But he's only five. Tell me you put shit on your kids' heads. Tell me. Maybe I'll feel better. You put shit on your patients' heads. You know that? Oh, you bastard. That's really funny. Hey, why did you get your hair cut? Why don't you let it grow? Looks dumb with a beard and short hair. What do you think of my painting? Hey, dumb-dumb. You there?

It goes this way. The sky is up above. I had it resting sideways when I left it last session. You set it back the same way, unless you didn't move it for a week, which is unlikely. Maybe it should be with the sky below and the darkness up above. It's all falling down. The dumb painting is cold. Cold as it is outside. The gesso cracks and I really like it when it does that. Those schmoo shaped things, they look like uteri coming out of her vagina. They're all falling out. Just dropping. Whap. I can't stand it that way. Go

95

to hell. I should have brought up two other paintings. They are in the car. They're crummy. I did them a long while ago. Did them with gesso, too, and ink. This one took maybe twenty minutes to do. And it represents three months work. I haven't painted in a long time.

It doesn't do any good, doc, it just doesn't. . . . I'm pissed at you, you bastard. I'll throw my painting at you. It doesn't help me one bit to paint. I still feel crappy. I have one I inked over and over and over and over, until it works. I'll bring that one in. It's different. Very dark. A different kind of thing. See, but once they're out . . . when I say out . . . I mean once they're out of me, out there . . . it's just like . . . it's just like Gil, it's just like the thing in the prophet, it comes through me. But it's not of me. I mean it's . . . it's on its own now. It belongs to whomever looks at it. And recreates it for himself or herself, as well as me.

I'm a spectator of it now. Which I believe is also a creative process. To . . . ahh . . . for the whole esthetic thing to work. Both the person who does it, called the artist, and the person who looks at it, or reads it, or listens to it, or sees it on the film; if it's all gonna work, the spectator has to go through his own creative thing. It may be totally different. To come up with a totally different . . . it doesn't matter. Each of us may be different. But the creative process is there. And that's how I am with these things once they're done. Now some things are not done. Some things are rotten and I throw them out, after they sit around for a long time. Or I hang them up, or I stick them up in the painting room, 'cause I don't like them anymore. They're icky. And there's not much else I can do with them. But some hang around and gnaw at me. They are icky and awful.

Part of it is that I don't like to spend money on canvases. So I work on it again. And again and again. And sometimes I wind up having to throw it out, and sometimes they work in a peculiar way. This painting—the one I brought in last week—just came out. One of those fast jobbies. See, I don't think it's weird, odd, a cop-out or in any way peculiar to paint it one way and to hang it upside down. I've always done that since I've painted. I wonder sometimes if I should have a circular thing to rotate them. Like with my feelings. With my guts. Turn them upside down.

EIGHT

MY FEELINGS, THEIR FEELINGS

HEY, THAT'S NICE. DONE IN PEN and ink. One of your patients give it to you? It's about time you got something decent to hang up on your walls. I wanted to ask you something. In the *group*, on Tuesday, was I receiving bad vibes from you? See, I felt uncomfortable in the *group* because I thought I was playing my old game. It's hard for me to know just how much of it's games and how much of it's sincere feelings when I say positive things to people. And especially because I'm really scared in the *group* because of the new people. And it is my habit always to throw in praise, to say nice things to people . . . when they're not in my family. I feel the nice things I say, but why it bugs me is that I seldom say the not-nice things that I also will feel from time to time. And so I was uncomfortable with my own self at that point.

I tend to knock you a lot. And it's for a number of reasons. One reason is that I don't consider you a participant in the *group*. I've said that before. You do your own technique or whatever it is. You aren't a real person in *there*, usually. So my responses to you are like my responses to tables and chairs. Then on the other hand, a lot of them in *there* . . . especially, well maybe not especially, but Grace will sometimes indicate you're all God. And I think that's a bunch of crap. I've been there before, and I know how much crap that is. No shrink is God. Not even you, though at times I've wondered if you really could separate the Potomac.

I don't like the God thing they feel about you. I don't

like that whole feeling. A bunch of neurotic women sitting around, and here's you—the male. So I tend to knock what Grace says you said to her. Or her attitude, that you've said her family's nice. Well, her family shits on her. I really don't care whether they do drop dung on her or whether you think they're nice. From her point of view, they shit on her all the time. I think one has to deal with that. It was in that context that I felt I was getting bad vibes from you. At this very moment . . . into my head comes the, uhm . . . thought that I accepted what Grace said you said as being what you said. So that could be a mistake. Did you tell her that? I think you did. Maybe not. Maybe you didn't. I tend to assume too much, right? I buy that. I'm new at checking things out. When somebody says the Pope just got married, I take their word for it. It's just a natural response. That's something new—to question it. That perhaps so and so got it wrong, shades of accuracy. But maybe, you know, uhm . . . maybe the Pope just got engaged. And me, I believe he got married.

Is it possible for me to feel bad vibes from you when, in fact, they might be from whatever part of me that felt I should be getting bad vibes from you? Goddamn it, you're frustrating. I think sometimes I just bounce off my own self. Like I put onto you my feelings, project them onto you from me, when they aren't you at all. I put it out there, or on you, and then bounce off it by using you or somebody else as, oh, gee, maybe it's them sending me bad vibes. But it's really me sending me bad vibes.

'Cause, I do feel, especially with the new people . . . I immediately had what I used to have a lot on. . . . I'm going to tell you . . . I used to have envies a lot on certain kinds of women. A lot. Attractive, slender, articulate, sophisticated, bright women would intimidate the shit out of me. It hasn't happened for a long time. I don't think I've come up against any of them lately. And I started having that on one of the new ladies you added to the *group*. What's her name—uhm, Noreen. And so I said what I thought were nice things to her or agreeable things like, yea, you're not alone out there, or at least I wanted to say nice things. And I thought to myself, you mean you're just doing that to be nice. I didn't know . . . what I said was true . . . she is a very sophisticated . . . everybody feels similar to that in their own individual stylistic way, having just started group therapy when the others of us know each other better.

I'm only concerned with why I said it. Whether I said it because—yea, that's so. Or I wanted to purge myself of the envies. Or to prevent what Grace and I were talking about . . . any rejection or any bad things from somebody out there. Noreen could put me right. . . . The other new lady, Linda, the one who's a religion fanatic, she doesn't scare me. At the end of the session when I said, Linda, you're smiling, I really felt that. I don't look much at the women during the time, except if I'm talking to somebody. I don't . . . when somebody's talking I don't look around and see what everybody else is doing . . . or showing. There's just too many people to do that. Well, when I looked up, and this woman who'd been crying since she was five years old wasn't crying, I thought that was, you know for the moment, just terrific. But as my words came out, I thought, oh, there you go again. This lady earlier told me I contradicted myself. I don't agree with her. I don't think I did. I was angry at her, and still I said a nice thing to her. I thought, you know, you're getting into the good graces of this lady so you won't be so scared. See, with Margaret, I don't do that with Margaret, 'cause when I talk to Margaret, I'm almost not talking to Margaret at all. I'm talking to Jeff.

Well, anyway, those were the silent things that were going on in my head, as other things were taking place. They don't make me too crazy. I'm just at one little step of awareness at it. I don't know. It's just a little bit of crap. What I've got to do is start somewhere in sorting out my feelings. What I'm doing right in here with you isn't crap. What I'm doing in thinking about it as I wash the dishes or clean the dog shit, that's not crap. How can

I say it? The experience of it in *there*, in the *group*, on Tuesday, that's a little bit of crap. Just a little bit.

So how do I get better? How do I get away from the confused feelings? The re-experiencing is terribly important, both in the *group* and the carry-over feelings when I redo it inside my head, as I am cleaning up the dishes or cleaning up the dog's shit, or whatever I'm cleaning up. I hear all these mixed messages between me and me. That within my own self, I must learn what is purely me, what is me bouncing off others, and what messages really come from others. All of these feelings differ from crossed communications between Jeff and me. . . . Am I right?

For a male chauvinist pig, you're not a bad shrink. Even if you ain't what I'd call exactly friendly at times.

NINE

GOING ALL AROUND TO SAY IT STRAIGHT

WHEN? WHAT'S TODAY? THURSDAY. On Tuesday
night I had . . . uhm, an interesting experience with
Jeffy. We had one of the familiar go arounds. We started
talking about charitable causes. We got one of those
Common Cause letters, and we were rapping about that.
We don't join things, and we don't sent money to anybody 'cause we don't have it to send. But this . . . I
. . . uhm . . . I asked Jeff, out of anybody, forgetting the
difficulties in getting nominated and getting elected and all
that garbage, who would you like to see president? And
he mentioned Gardner, and I said, oh, we got this thing in
the mail today, and we read through this junk and thought
about it. The Cause had mentioned Gardner, see. When
we started talking about this, it started snowballing in a
zillion different directions, mostly . . . uhm . . . what a
crummy bitch I am . . . except recently. There was some
lip service paid to *recently*. Like, I've been a little nicer.
Not yelling so much and seeing that his coffee is ready in
the morning. Stuff like that.

There was such pain in this man's eyes. You know, he
came back from Peru. These trips just tear his aching guts
out. If he didn't have the tranquilizers, he'd never make it.
Because . . . uhm. . . . He was in his hotel, and he heard
this big explosion, and he thought, huh, the revolution.
And he went outside, and there were millions of people
in the streets. And he finally found out the explosions were
firecrackers, and it was a religious thing. They were carry-

103

ing the Cardinal, or the Bishop, or whoever the hell it was, down the street, and these poor slobs had come . . . they had been walking two weeks. They haven't got a pot to pee in. They haven't got anything, and their life expectancy is age thirty-five. And they are buying this rotten religious junk from the vendors in the street and throwing flowers and money to this . . . this ass. And Jeff, in telling me, just broke down. He couldn't stand it. He goes down there, you know, to bring sophisticated scientific knowledge to the Chairman of Health, who walks around with a sword in his goddamn hip, because he's an idiot, right? And it tears Jeff's guts out.

Anyway . . . in this talk we had Tuesday night, we just went 'round and 'round, and I only get defensive in these kinds of talks. It was just crazy. And I thought, oh, shit. 'Cause I had spoken some about what I thought was happening to me in *group* therapy and in therapy in general. And most of that comes across to him as selfish shit. Like he's thinking, I'm out trying to make a living, and I gotta face this kind of garbage. So this goes 'round and 'round and nothing's taking place, except I'm thinking, terrific, every time I think I'm making headway, I get shit thrown in my face. It never fails.

But I kept my mouth shut pretty much. Somehow I kept the defenses down. And last night, I thought what the hell. I'm gonna pop one of these lovely little green pills, that I manipulated you into prescribing for me. Bet you didn't know that. But once you gave them to me, I didn't take them for three days. The game was over, right? So I didn't have to take them. But I did take one one day, which was hysterical. Hey, I gotta tell you something in parentheses for a minute. I was just really getting irritable. It was over the weekend. Oh, I was just suddenly—BOOM! I was . . . just like this. It was around dinner time, and I could hear the screams coming. So I popped one of these, and five minutes after nearly screaming at everybody and telling them all to go to hell, Cindy was tasting something, and I was calling the dog, which is usually, come here, you stupid-son-of-a-bitch dog. Well, I said, Hercules, dear, come into the kitchen. And Cindy nearly cracked up, falling on the floor laughing. And I started getting the sillies. From this little green goody. It was terrific. And Cindy said, give me one of those. I want those. And I said, no.

So I decided I wasn't going to go to the Tuesday night thing at the *Art Patch*, and about five-thirty, which is about forty-five minutes before Jeff gets home, I'm gonna pop one of these, and I'll let the chemicals do their work. And maybe I won't get defensive. I'll just play the game. I'll make sure everything's quiet, and there's ice in the bucket for his drink, and I'll have to organize it so Gil has eaten, and then he'll bathe, and then the dog shit will be wiped up and all this stuff. And so I did this thing.

I kept it going for about an hour thinking, oh-oh, I'm gonna puke in a minute. And Jeff's sitting in the rocking chair saying, it's really nice to see you so cheerful. I thought what he wants is a mannequin. So what. A wind-up doll! But lo and behold, this man who walks around with his eyes . . . there's something wrong with his eyes right now, literally . . . it started happening right before he left on this trip. And it happened there. Some doctor there gave him some junk. His eyes get incredibly red. When he wakes up in the morning, they are sealed shut with gluck. But one time it happened to him really bad. And it was when we were leaving Boston, and he was visiting Rosenberg a couple of times. And Rosenberg said, well, he said everything was psychosomatic, but that . . . that the cause was that Jeff wanted to cry, and he wouldn't cry. The whole thing of leaving Boston and all the symbolism related to leaving.

And it's true that in Peru, that's how he felt. So there's . . . there's some . . . anyway, looking at his eyes, all sad and red and painful, as we talked very quietly . . . he talked to me about dialogue and stuff and how he and I must have dialogue. And one of the things he says to me is that you want to know Grace. I think maybe I told you that I mentioned Grace several times to him. He said, I want you to want to know me that way. And on one level while he's talking, I'm thinking about his jealousy of Gilly and a lady he doesn't even know. So we got into this thing. And I'm under the influence of this little pill.

And I'm saying to myself, don't open your mouth. But I did. It was sort of like . . . this is going to sound cold, but it was like a final or a mid-term exam—what have you learned from group therapy up until now? And I just talked, which I'd never really done before, the way we women talk in the *group*—straight. About him. Now I've played analyst to him before. But not on purpose, so this was a little different. In terms of how he comes across to people . . . to use a term of a friend of ours . . . he gets no reality feedback from anybody ever. Except from a few of our friends over the past. But certainly not in his profession. They are all scared shitless of him. Or they hate him or they . . . a lot love him, or it's all of these emotions. But there's no straight stuff. And I find it enormously difficult to give him straight stuff because . . . how it ended up . . . see Jeffy is very proud of where he is and the things he does.

He gave a symposium yesterday, and he felt terrific, and he was really proud of himself. So if he comes in and he says, I'm really proud, and everybody says, that's great, or Jeff says, I took a good trip, or I had a successful trip, and somebody says, that's great, be that somebody me or even Cindy . . . well . . . his response is, they don't have any understanding of the agony, or the shit and the pain and the garbage, that I go through, right? If he talks about the garbage and the shit, and we say, oooh, that sounds bad, why don't you change your job, then he'll switch another way. And I went on and on in this vein. Like, you know, he all of a sudden becomes the martyr or the original Jewish mother.

And it was sinking in. He kept saying, wow. Wow. It's beautiful, it's profound. You're coming through. I went on, the trouble is I can say apples to you, and you'll respond in such a different way . . . or you'll respond bananas. Then I'll say bananas, and you'll respond to apples or something else. The trouble is that it's not possible for me to say apples and bananas separately or together. And he flipped on that, and it was really a good talk. And I was really understanding for the first time that the idea of respect for him is so important. And the little things, of seeing that he has his shirts and suits cleaned . . . and the coffee in the morning, and this week I've been going out in the mornings in my pajamas and coat to start his stupid car. Playing the servant wife or suburban wife. It means so much to him. It made him get well, because . . . well, this week anyway, I didn't resent it.

And I don't think I'm doing it out of guilty feelings from past deeds. No. Because I thought about that. You know, this morning I went out, and it's a Ford. Fords never start, right? So I went out, and I'm grinding this thing into the ground, and nothing's happening. So I came back in; and Jeff's in the shower, and I yell in, I couldn't start it. And he said, okay, let it go, I'll get it started. I went and had some coffee, and he was still in the shower, and I thought, oh, well, it's warmed up a little bit, I'll go out. And I went out and I got it started.

I came back in and he had seen what I'd done 'cause the bathroom window overlooks the driveway, and he said, I thought I told you not to start it. And I said, well, I went out and started it anyway. He said, you disobeyed me. And I said, go to hell. And we laughed. You know, it was really nice. It was just really nice. That's a perfect example of when I say apples and I mean bananas. Both Jeff and I know it. And we respond that way. And when the talk works out, it's a beautiful thing. The wires don't get crossed. But too often when he says let's play, and he means let's work, I hear let's play, because in that instance he says one thing, but means another, and I miss it. In those instances, the car doesn't start. Yea.

So there are the good moments when I catch what he throws, and he catches what I throw. These are times when neither of us sends simultaneous contradictory messages. Or if we do, we know it. When it is possible to receive a disguised message and recognize the disguise and respond to the real message. But it's hard. I'm just beginning to learn how to straighten communication with Jeff. You can see that I don't even do it in the *group* yet. Really. I'm only thinking about it. I've never been able to do that. I'm just sort of learning. And the *group* is helping. The *group's* terrific . . . like I was saying last session. Both of us must know, at least some of the time, that what we say is or is not what we mean. That is basic to all real communication between us. I hope I'm not wrong in assuming Jeff knows this. I hope I'm not pretending he sees it when he doesn't.

And with Gil . . . when was it? Last session, or the week before that, when I was rapping about Gilly . . . about putting shit on his head and stuff. Well, I calmed down, even before I started taking the little greenies. I've only taken three. Two or three. I just started calming down. Stopping screaming. But being straight and open when I'm angry. And Gil has had maybe five or six days of really good stuff. He's been calm. He hasn't been up-tight. And he's into the readiness programs . . . for the first time I see evidence that he's ready for the programs they throw at him in school. It was just really beautiful.

He was so funny Saturday night when Jeff came home. In the afternoon . . . it was Cindy's birthday. And I baked her a cake. She was so thrilled 'cause these guys called up who . . . they weren't going to come over because they didn't have a car. Then they got hold of a car. This guy and his girl friend and his roommate came over, and she was just so happy when they came over and ate. And I baked this cake . . . and they were in the . . . with the candles going in the living room and all this garbage. And I was

108

going to bed. Jeff had fallen asleep, and I heard Gil call. He had called Cindy to come up. And she went up. And I went up and asked what's going on? And he said, when is she going to bed? And I said, well, she's seventeen now. She can stay up late and entertain her friends. And he stuck his head in the pillow and said, oooh, when am I going to be seventeen? This five year old little kid! He's just too much. And then we talked about how neat it was to be five. He's just great.

TEN

THE SON OF ZEUS

SPOOKY WAS REALLY A MESS. Our new dog, for all
his shitting and pissing around, is really a good dog because,
when he's angry he just goes *GRUFFT* like that! You know,
he lets you know, damn it, play with me, or do something
with me. And he's just a really neat dog. Much nicer than
Spooky was. This Hercules is just a neat dog. We named
him after our friends, the Hortons. They had this most noble
beast of all. They found him at the shelter a zillion years
ago. They must have had him for maybe twelve years.
He was part great dane and boxer, and had this huge
noble head. Oh, he was just a marvelous beast.

When Jeff would write . . . when Jeff would travel, he
would never write to Clara or Dick, he'd write to Hercules.
And when we went round and round for four hours to
name the shepherd, we finally decided . . . I said, you gotta
name him Hercules because old Hercules is gonna die.
I said, Clara told me Hercules was old and sick, and he
was gonna die.

Well, funny thing, a few days later, Jeff called up the
Hortons. And sure enough, old Herc had died just before
Christmas. And it really touched Jeff so much. Oh, he
was . . . just so . . . he was just really happy that I had
said that, and that the line was to be carried on. And this
dog is really a neat Hercules. He's gonna be three hundred
pounds and four feet tall. He's just a neat dog. The second
in the generation of noble beasts. And he and Gil have a
neater thing than Gilly had with Spook. So that's nice.
And he's smart. He's a smarter dog. Even though he won't

111

get housebroken. If you have any suggestions along that line, I'd like to hear them. I haven't taken him to the vet yet. Not until he's ten weeks old. Who do you take your dog to? Huh? I'm not going back to that old bastard that we took Spooky to.

Jeff was really touched by the death of Hercules I. Yes. Moved. He was saddened. I don't think he realized . . . he wasn't around when Clara said . . . we saw them last summer . . . that Hercules was really getting old and sick. And the fact, when Jeff called, that Hercules had died; the fact that I had said he was gonna die—it wasn't any ESP—I knew the dog was sick and old and was gonna die. And he was sad that he couldn't write to Hercules anymore, and I said, well, yea, you can. You can write to our Hercules. And that made him feel better. He gets into these little moments.

I . . . it was really hard to name this dog. We couldn't seem to hit on a name that fit him. At first, before the phone call, the name Hercules didn't seem to fit him. And I always did like the name Spooky, and I kept calling him Spook. Like, you know, mixing it up. At first we were going to call him Kodiac, because he looked like a bear. And his mother's name was Bear. But it didn't seem to fit him, and we finally settled on Hercules, 'cause Hercules was gonna die. So Jeff said, that's it. We're gonna call this dog Hercules. So, when the Hortons told him that, he was really into this thing about old Hercules, you know . . . right? Hercules is dead.

No, I don't feel bad about old Hercules. He lived a really good life, except when Dick used to beat him. He was like a person, and I think ours will be like that. I mean this is our third try at an animal. On a dog animal. We've had a zillion turtles to die. And Gil has got to believe that our animals do live after all. I think this one will work out. He seems healthy enough. He's already grown like three inches. He's all black except for a white patch on his chest, and his ears stick up. I'm talking an awful lot about this dog, because I spend a lot of time with this stupid animal. I'm the one who gets up in the morning and feeds him. I'm the one who cleans the kitchen floor, and takes him out to run him, and takes him out after he eats so that he'll shit out there. And keeps him out of everybody's hair when they don't want to be bothered.

It's driving me crazy. And I get very angry about it. But he happens to be a neat animal. I figure sooner or later I'll get some reward for it. Like he'll protect me against some monsters. And he's a good addition to the family. He likes me—even though I beat him. What can he do? I also feed him. He's neat. He comes to me. He brings a little toy to me. He's only seven weeks old. But he still shits and pees in the kitchen. And on the rug, too, if you give him a chance. How did you keep your dog from shitting in the house? For you it's probably no problem. Your dog would never, never dream of doing such a thing. Probably doesn't even have a rectum. Either that or your dog poops milk chocolate. Yea, it has to be. You really do walk on water, right? Now I've got the sillies, and I didn't even take one of your little greenies.

Next week when you're with the patient before me . . . if you hear the sound of an elephant walking, you'll know I decided to bring Hercules. Say, that's wild. Think of the millions that would applaud me because they think shrinks are for the dogs.

Eleven

HEY, DIDDLE—DIDDLE

ANYBODY WHO'D DRIVE IN THIS SNOW is crazy. If I wasn't convinced before that I need a shrink, I am now. You have a drink for an old friend? I don't feel friendly. Actually I'm on an anti-Becky kick, because I didn't like that shrink remark in the *group* . . . you made that shrink remark to me last Tuesday, and don't give me any of your usual stuff about how I don't read you and all that shit. I wasn't acting like a shrink, and you know it. I don't even know how to act like a shrink. Who'd want to? So why'd you say that? I took offense at that. I took offense at that whole meeting . . . the whole . . . it wasn't horrible until you opened your mouth. I didn't understand what was going on. Maybe you could explain to me why you said that—before I defend myself.

Did you feel I was callously probing by the way I asked the ladies questions? Your calling me . . . saying I was acting like a shrink implied I didn't care about the answers anyway. Asking questions just to talk. Well, damn, I gotta know what these people are like on their insides if I'm gonna dump my shit out there. I have to know who they are. Maybe Helen can sit there and . . . she has known Irene a few more months than I have. Maybe she can say Irene is with it. I don't know Irene from beans. I haven't the faintest idea what that woman feels. Whether that's my bag, 'cause I can't read the mysterious sphinx . . . I don't know.

But when those women open their mouths and let loose, I don't know what the hell's going on with them. All I see

115

is my image of them. So what is that? It is no good if I'm going to relate to my image of them. That's what I do all the time anyway. That's what I don't want to do. See, I'm not saying you put me down, even though I'm pissed at you. Maybe it is true. Maybe in the last analysis, I don't give a damn about those people, and if I ask about them, it's callously probing. And maybe, also, because I didn't want to talk about me. Questioning them is one way for me to avoid talking about me. And that whole thing, when you said right in the *group* on Tuesday that I was a part of the triad with Grace and Helen of cliquish nonsense, of . . . I mean they've been doing that since I've been in there. So what.

It's always going on. The women in the *group* are always going to talk about ladies that used to be in the *group*, and aren't now. So this time, Grace and Helen and I did. Big deal. If it bugs somebody, as sometimes it's bugged me, I ask what are you talking about? Who was that? What was so and so like a few months ago or last year? You know, I suppose . . . uhm . . . this is gonna sound petty, and all of that, but this is what I feel. You're . . . super, super protective of these two new women in the *group*. Well, damn it, Noreen and Linda made tremendous decisions in their lives. If they don't know what so and so's talking about, then they can ask. You never protected me that way when I was new. You tossed me in. That's all. Swim, Pam, old girl, you said. And I'm fed up because you still do that to me. You even hang remarks on me, like that shrink remark. Now I know, maybe I'm . . . getting into all your techniques, and maybe this is playing shrink. Okay. But it pissed me.

Perhaps I should try to say in the *group* what I say to you alone in here. No, I couldn't. It was just really weird. Maybe it was because I felt so uncomfortable in there the last few weeks. Really weird . . . I don't know . . . I . . . I didn't realize until after I left on Tuesday that it was one of the few times that I didn't go through a whole big thing

116

while I was driving down here—thinking about what's bugging me and how to say it. I just totally blocked it. So totally that maybe that's why I asked people questions. I don't usually do that.

If they wanna rap, they can rap. And I didn't realize until afterward, you know, that there are two or three things that are bugging me in my personal life. Well, I . . . I just didn't feel . . . uhm . . . I just didn't trust the whole place enough to dump it. So what. I figured it was trivia. That I could handle it. I don't know . . . it's so. . . . So I might as well dump it here. Now.

Cindy's gonna be leaving, probably on the fifteenth of the month. She wanted to . . . as soon as she feels it's the time to go, she wants to leave right then. I'm sad about it. And there isn't anybody to talk to about it being sad. Jeff doesn't want to hear about my sadness. Cindy knows that I'm sad. Yea. I told her. I told her I was gonna miss her. But beyond that, what am I gonna say to her? I'm sad. So I said it. There's nothing else to say. I mean that's okay.

She and I were rapping. And I was talking about something about my father, and she said, oh, yea, good old Pop-Pop, he used to diddle me when I was a little girl, and I thought it was sort of strange, and I mentioned it to Mom, and Mom told Mom-Mom. That's what my sister had Cindy call my parents. And from then on, my sister said that Cindy shouldn't be alone with that old shit. Those were thoughts I always had about my father. But for somebody to come out and tell me. . . .

It made me sick. It made me want to puke. It made me want to cry and scream. I don't know. Old men diddle little girls all the time, I guess. I've heard about it before. I guess it just makes me sick that it was my father. Jeff didn't understand that. Oh, I don't know if he understood that or not. He teased me about it, and that hurt me a lot. I left the room. And it was a curious thing because, uhm . . . the next day we were sitting in the living room rapping, and he said, you're a true intellectual. He knows this is one of my buzz words, as they call it in his game. He said, you've gotten yourself together so much, in so many ways. And then he said, there are these little things like your old man diddling your niece when she was little, and that will set you off. Those weren't his exact words.

And, yea, Cindy remembered that. With no feeling. No feeling. I mean she wasn't upset about it. She's a fairly stoic kid. It takes a lot to get a tear out of that kid. I don't think she remembers it with any . . . I don't know how she remembers it. She just laid it out. I've known. . . .

My friend, Connie, in New York used to do that. Her brother used to fuck her all the time. You know, make her suck him when she was little. Nine. She used to lay it out, in every shrink's office across the . . . wherever she went. She'd just lay it out, with no feeling. And I used to hear it, and it used to tear me up. Connie's not alone in that either. You know, little Sara, not my sister, Sara, but the one who used to baby-sit for us, told me that her brother screwed her too. At least it bugged her, a little bit. But she likes her brother! She sticks up for him all the time. He's some ass who's got some girl knocked-up, and now's twenty-two, and is a cook, and, you know, has four children. She doesn't . . . Sara doesn't baby-sit for us now. Not anymore. She got married. Abruptly. To some creep who turned out to be a syphilitic, without telling her.

Morally sick. These situations are always sick. But I don't know. I don't know what's real and what's not real. I get upset. But the people who have it happen to them don't seem to get upset. I do. Just hearing about it. And Cindy really knows what she means, when she says Pop-Pop diddled her. She said, he finger-fucked me. Those were Cindy's words. She just told me. I didn't ask her, either. She just told me. She told me without any recognizable feeling. Well, I corroborated with Nancy. She's the one I told who's my neighbor, and we went to the museum with the kids. Remember? Well, I talked to her because it seemed strange to me. But it's not unusual. It's not unique. I . .

118

I mean . . . if that had happened to me . . . my grandfather
. . . if I'd ever known him, and he'd done it to me, and
I'd blocked it out, it would seem like it would tear my gut
everytime I thought about it. Especially if it's something
I never disremembered. I don't know. There it was. Now
I can't . . . I read her . . . I mean I've just seen Cindy cry
a little bit. When I say cry, I mean show . . . uhm . . .
what? It's not that she's cold. She's not. It is just that she's
fairly stoic. It drives my sister up the wall.

Like when my mother died. Rosalie is fifteen. You remember me telling you about Rosalie, Cindy's sister. She went
into her hysterics. Well, that's Rosalie with her hysterical
thing. And Cindy does her . . . uhm . . . down-to-earth
realistic thing. She loved my mother. A lot. But that's the
way it is. People live. And they die. I remember my sister
felt strange about it. She felt Cindy was holding it all in.
Not letting out. It's true, Cindy holds a lot in, 'cause she
doesn't trust anybody. Or she'll laugh at scarey situations.
That's kind of standard teenage stuff. It's new for her with
guys. Everything is new for her.

What bothered me is that Jeffy didn't know that it really
upset me. Like he's accepted how crazy, shitty his parents
are. Why haven't I? Well, who wants to do that? Yea, I
know my parents were crazy, shitty. But I don't have to
think about it all the time. I don't have to have evidence
presented to me all the time. And just say, well, they're
crazy or shitty or sick or dumb or whatever. Then, there
could be the other side. That Cindy didn't experience the
diddling as unpleasant at all. There's a really good chance
she didn't find it unpleasant. But I respond in expectation
that she should have felt revulsion or horror or something
really bad.

Because . . . well . . . I would have as a little girl. But
she's grown up in a different world. So maybe now little
girls don't feel that way. I don't know. I was scared shitless
of my father. I didn't know whether it was him or my
mother. I always believed it was my mother who did that

119

to me. She was an expert at laying a lot of taboo shit on me, and sexual stuff was one example. She'd say never, never kiss your father on the mouth, Pam. You'll get germs. Well, then I thought it was really peculiar when I was kissing strange little boys on the mouth. How come I couldn't kiss my father on the mouth? So now I wonder, maybe my mother knew something I didn't know. I don't know. . . .

It never occurred to me until Cindy said that. I guess it did occur to me, but I wasn't gonna . . . I don't want to dig into that. . . . That's my father's bag. Not mine. And I don't see him but once a year or less, so I don't want to worry about it. I told you he remarried about three months ago, didn't I? Terrific, he's got a wife he can screw now. The old bastard. Here I was, crying and feeling sad because I didn't have the money to fly to New York for his wedding. And when I called, after agonizing about it for months and months . . . when I finally called to say I was sorry, he told me he hadn't expected or wanted or thought much about me coming anyway. Real casual like. I just was double . . . double upset about what Cindy told me, because Jeffy didn't seem to know why I couldn't laugh at it. You know, like we laugh at his mother, or some of his relatives . . . his mother who thinks she's a saint.

See, I grew up with enormous fantasies about my father. I always thought . . . I . . . I didn't . . . I don't remember his being around very much. And I just felt that my mother was a big dominant bitch, who didn't let him be his own self. And I thought she was always in the way. That's why I was so hostile toward her. You know I went for three years in therapy rapping about this crap. It spilled out up to the ceiling in the therapy room. It was the standard Jewish scene . . . with the woman whose presence is there with a capital P, and the husband who goes out and putters, just to get the hell out. And, and . . . who's thought of as a piece of shit. You know the story. If my

120

mother hadn't gone to work, we'd have never had the house, and bla, bla, bla, and on and on and on. 'Cause Daddy's a lazy schmuck. Okay, he's not the, uhm . . . your typical Jewish merchant who makes a lot of money. Terrific. And I hated her. I thought it was her. So I spent a lot of time in my therapy with the other shrinks rapping . . . talking about her. This sort of thing.

In later years I thought, well, maybe it wasn't only her. Maybe part of it was him. Maybe that's how she saw him, or that's how he was, or she made her decisions the way she felt she had to make her decisions. See, it was all tied up in mother's going to work, which I hated her for. For doing that . . . leaving me. She claimed she had to do that in order to provide me with a better physical environment and nicer kids to play with than my sister had. 'Cause my father wasn't pulling in that kind of bread. It gets all mixed up, and I don't want to go into all this all over again. Once in awhile, I suppose something keys it all off in me. Those things are never purged in therapy. They're just understood to a certain degree and learned to live with. That's all. They're still there. See, I used to think I couldn't relate to him because big, fat Ma-Ma was in the way. Like she kept me at a distance from him.

Well, when big, fat Ma-Ma died, I still couldn't relate to the man. And that's why I was so upset about the wedding. I thought, well, maybe I could reach my father through the wedding. It wouldn't have worked. Deep inside, I knew it wouldn't have worked. And I'm tired of trying to relate to him. The old finger-fucker. I don't want to relate to those people. I've got other things and another family to think about. But once in awhile, something is said that brings the whole thing back to me. I'm playing it down now because that's where I think it needs to be. Maybe that's why I didn't bring any of this up in the *group,* because . . . what for? It's just some left over drag, as Rosenberg would say.

And it's only significant in so far as I just wanted Jeff to recognize that once in awhile the drag comes to me and bugs me. And once in awhile the drag comes to him and bugs him. Less often perhaps to him, but it comes. It comes when his stupid spiteful mother sells his father's tools to those ass-hole relatives. And that's all the old man left Jeff. The bitch hates her two sons so much that she won't even give them an old wrench. Why do mothers and fathers do a lot of evil things? I find that scarey as you know, because I'm a mother. And it's not for nothing that *mother* is often used as a swear word among blacks. Okay. That's enough of that. . . . Don't give me your sighs and junk. It's not important. It's not important. I insist it's not important in my life! And you can sigh all you want, I'm not going to talk about that left-over drag.

It seems like I always come out of this building on Tuesday hating your guts, and I always come back here on Thursday and still trust you enough anyway. I find that incredible. I suppose it still always is that you're two people for me. Maybe that's because, in the *group,* I have jealousies. I don't know. I hate that. I hate that in me. That's why I call you chauvinist a lot. 'Cause I hate it in me. To be jealous of you because of these two new women in the *group* is crazy. Not with the other women. That's weird that I never felt that way about them. That's one of the things I always thought I would feel. That's why I shied away from *groups.* Now I'm regressing into the wingding that he's my shrink, not yours, like in the past with my previous therapy, when I would go out different doors, never to see other patients, and carry on that stupid myth.

Well, until these two new gals came in, I hadn't experienced that here. I don't like it. It's ugly. Just vomitous. And because I'm. . . . There's one thing I'm not learning in *there.* I'm not learning. . . . I'm not. . . . I don't know the right word. Maybe it's *knowing.* I'm not *knowing* those people. I was always bad at sizing people up. I still am. I'm incredibly poor at that. That's why I was such a bad social worker. I couldn't tell a chiseler from a man starving to death. I never could. Used to get sucked in all the time by people who were shrewder than I. On the other hand, Jeff has this tremendously accurate capacity to size people up immediately, to know them immediately. I remember once, some weeks ago, when Maxine didn't show up for the *group,* and you said something about, maybe she could be drinking. And Irene said, I don't know her well enough to know if she could be drinking, and you said very loud, you don't know her. Well, who knows her?

Maxine sits in there . . . how long has she been in there . . . a zillion years . . . and she says, I have a drinking problem. And every time I ask her, what causes you to drink, Helen pipes up and says, oh, not again—we've been through that already. Well, obviously not, if she tells us she's gonna quit therapy and you tell her she'll start drinking again in two months. Obviously not. People don't have drinking problems. They booze it because they got other problems. That's all. Or they take heroin or they eat. Or they do all kinds of compulsive, shitty things. And all the crap on television about alcoholism being a disease is just garbage. As though, you know, they went out and caught a virus. Or obesity, or any of those stupid things.

They are existential illnesses, if you want to call them that. People are responsible for them. And by that, I mean it's not that the world hasn't pushed individuals that way. But those people are responsible for finding out what it was that pushed them, either from the inside or from the outside. And if Irene says she doesn't know Maxine, then Maxine obviously hasn't told Irene who she is. Or any of us for that matter. And see, I have to wait for three months after the session it happened in before I figure out what's going on. Three months later—now I respond to that. Those things stick in my head. And it takes me . . . this time . . . months to tell you what I thought about your jumping on Irene. I couldn't say it then. I didn't know enough, in my own head.

You awake back there? What are you doing? Picking your nose or something? I wonder if you snore. I want to be angry with you. But I'm not. I'm just angry, and if I gotta be angry at somebody, you're a good choice. So I'll think of you referring to me as a shrink, because then I bristle. It's a bad word. It's a word I never used to use. I used to think it was disgusting. I wish I could find another word. Shrinks don't shrink heads. Good ones don't anyway. They expand heads . . . to help you to grow. It's hard to be mad at you when I'm not. Try harder, Pam, she said to herself, you've got to have more angries than that. I told you I was angry. But I haven't given anything but *hug you's* all day. You bastard. I told you what I was angry about. You called me a shrink. You said, all you older girls in the *group* are cutting out my two little new sweeties, who are afraid to pee unless I tell them.

Listen. That Noreen can hold her own fine. There is a strong lady there. Now there's one of my fast judgments. In three months, I'll come back and say, oh, that lady's falling apart. Linda, with all her Catholic guilts, is pretty tough, too, for all her crying. . . .

See, what I'm angry at is me. 'Cause I'm too chicken-shit to go in there and say, look, you're an ass, or say, look, Grace, for weeks you haven't said anything that amounts to a pile of piss. I don't suppose piss can be piled, but those metaphores come to mind because of Hercules. I'm too scared to go in there and say, you're full of crap. Who am I to say that? I guess the only one I've ever said it to is Margaret. I don't know why. Except I think I've been to those places. Not as much as she has. And not as forever as she is. Margaret is back on her black cloud again. Why should I find out? I don't know Margaret. What is Margaret to me? What are any of those people to me? You know, I pay you in order to sit and talk with them. What is that? Something's wrong with the system when that has to happen. Sigmund Freud and his buddies can go suck themselves. Jung is cross-eyed, and I don't like him anyway.

Listen, why can't I say what I want in the *group*? Am I afraid they're gonna blast me? So, what if they don't like me. Maybe it has to do with my feelings about you. My jealousy of you? You're not gonna like me if I pour shit on some little chicky in *there?* Yea, well that's kind of the feeling I got. Tuesday, that was the message you were sending me, I thought. Oh, I don't know. I think I'll have to sit farther away from you in the *group.* Sitting right next to you is tough. Maybe I'll sit across from you. I'll get a different perspective that way. Somehow I've got to see you in my special way, no matter what. Oh, balls! I don't know. Maybe if I wear sunglasses, you'll look the way I want you to. Maybe you should go stick your head in the toilet.

I can't help it. I've this bottomless need to paint you one color in the *group* and a different color in individual therapy. And look, you old. . . . I'm trying to make the two join together. In here, I'd paint you red, gold, yellow: soft and warm and living colors. I'd paint you human and friendly in here, on Thursdays. I don't like you on Tuesdays! You're baby-shit brown in *there.* You're either nobody, Mr. Nobody, or you're Mr. Puppeteer. Neither one is very pleasant.

That's not to say it isn't helpful. I don't know if it's helpful or not. Kind of like your office door—helpful. There's just something I gotta do in that *group,* and I just have to do it. I'm not exactly sure what it is, or how. But I'm not right in that *group.* I haven't been feeling and thinking right for a long time in *there.* And it's because I'm . . . I don't know. . . . I'm just scared. I've let them see my despair, but there's other parts of me I haven't let them see. Well, they've seen it, but I haven't consciously put it out. It feels mucky in *there.* I don't know for sure if it's the new people. I focus on them, but maybe it's Grace. In the back of my mind, there's Grace floating around. In the beginning weeks, she was the one for me who got through the muck and mire to nitty-gritty places. And she hasn't done that for a long time with anybody, except two weeks ago when she gave the poncho to Helen. That was really touching . . . to give a present to Helen in front of all of us. The rest of the time, she's about as laced up as an old-fashioned corset. I guess I'm just chicken-shit to tangle with Grace by telling her that.

I feel a fight coming, and that I'll be ganged-up on in *there*. Yea, yea. I get the feeling, like Irene said, that they all think I'm eloquent. I'm very glib. Terrific. Really verbal. All right. But that has nothing to do with responding to what people say. That often happens, as you know, as I've told you, months later with me. And it's that that bugs me. Makes me scared. I don't want the glibness to be there. I can either be glib, or I can shut up and withdraw, which is what I do when you lay some shit on me. And I don't want either of those. I want real stuff. The whole thing is really scarey. The fantasies . . . I feel like I'm in a mountain fantasy about this whole nonsense. I'm making a whole lot of stuff out of nothing. It's a really strange place. It's like being in Sleeping Beauty's castle in Disneyland; a big facade with no innards. Strange as hell. Jeff would say I'm crazy.

TWELVE

THE BALD TRUTH

I'M JUST NOWHERE. CINDY'S LEAVING in two weeks. So Cindy's off . . . leaving. I think Jeffy is glad she's going. I don't know. I sort of am, too, but I'm more ambivalent. Jeff finds her kind of a pain in the ass. He likes her, but she's kind of a pain in the ass. And he doesn't think that she pulls her own weight enough, which is probably true. He won't miss her, I will. He behaves like she robs him of me, but I don't think he knows that, or would even admit it if he did. Cindy and I can rap. She listens to me about things that Jeff doesn't. And Cindy can unload on me, too. It has really been nice. And Jeffy is right there again . . . or near there again . . . like when Gil was born. For all these years . . . this keeps going on with Jeff. Feels like I've said it a zillion times. Here I am, giving all the good stuff, or the best stuff, or whatever to Cindy. Not to Jeff. Or certainly less to Jeff. And when we get started talking about her, or any of her friends that come around, we usually get on the two sides of the fence. I'm generally sympathetic to teenagers and their plight, and he isn't. Or if he is being specific about Cindy, and I get very general and say that is what all teenagers do, he thinks it's a bunch of crap.

I had a funny dream. Remember I told you about Willy, the boy who lives up the street. He baby-sat for us during the summer, during the day. And his sister Sara is the one who used to sit for us at night when Jeff and I went to Spanish class. I used to get Willy to sit for Gil on Thursdays when I came to therapy, and then I would tool around.

127

Anyway, I hadn't seen Willy for a really long time. Since the first couple weeks that Cindy was here. So it was a couple months ago. Around Christmas. And I dreamed about him. We were in this big house, this huge house, where a lot of people . . . and I was really . . . well, I always am, anyway . . . very attracted to him. Except it didn't turn out good for him and me, because he and Cindy made it together.

Can you imagine that? She makes it with Willy, and I'm wandering around this house with all these people. And what's his name, this old man, that bald senator that I think is kind of sexy, what's . . . you know, he's on some special council . . . well, whatever. He was in the dream, too. It was all sort of funny. I'm attracted to this really old, bald senator and to Willy, who is seventeen. I'm sexually attracted to them in the dream. In the dream . . . and in real life both. Well, no, I'm not attracted to the senator; I just happen to think he's sexy. I think . . . thought General Eisenhower was sexy, too. I don't know, maybe I like bald men. I just think they're sexy; I don't know what it is. There's something about them. I like long hair, too.

The senator reminds me of Rubin Cohen, who was Mirium's husband. You know, the family I lived with when I was in school. Rubin was not quite as bald as the guy in the dream. But they had the same kind of face, and I always thought Rubin was sexy, too. I always liked Rubin. Willy is just adorable. I even have fantasies . . . waking sexual thoughts about him. I'd have to be dead not to like . . . be taken by him. Although Cindy thought he was kind-of-a-nothing. It's funny, because in real life she thought he was a creep, and in the dream, she makes it with him. It made me kind of mad, or jealous. Maybe both. I wonder if this has to do with her leaving to go back to her sister . . . I mean my sister . . . who is a bitch. Maybe I'm mad at Cindy in the dream, 'cause in real life, she's leaving. Prefers my sister to me. I don't know. I mean, she gets

128

Willy, and doesn't even like him, so I'm mad. Anyway, Willy and Cindy live in different worlds, in the real world. Willy is industrious in school and takes it all seriously. He is just smart. He's the only one in that stupid family of his that's going to get out of it. And he knows he needs them if he's going to get out of it. So he just plays it cool.

He's just smart, that's all. The others in the family are crazy. They scream and cry and do terrible things to each other just to make some kind of contact. He discovered he can't make contact with his parents, so he just cools it. Long hair bugs his father, so he doesn't grow long hair. The music bugs his father, so he plays it when his father's not home. To talk to Willy, you have to pull . . . he used to hang around after I would come home in the summer. I'd leave, say, at about eleven o'clock, go into Georgetown, tool around, and then come here, and then go home. I'd usually go in and get Gilly some ice cream and ask Willy if he wanted some, and he'd say, okay, yea. We'd sit around and shoot the shit.

It is difficult to talk to him because he's very quiet. If you ask him a question, he'll answer, but he doesn't offer anything on his own, generally. But he's really cute. And I haven't seen him in a long time. Besides, he's seventeen, and it's a whole . . . forget it. Curious that . . . I think it was curious that I dreamed about it, but I didn't consummate the deal. Cindy did; I thought that was sort of funny. See, there's this part of me that would like to . . . uhm . . . it's hard to come out and say it. Well, I figured that was . . . it had to do with the Oedipus thing with boys and mothers. There it was. So, in the dream, Cindy had to have him. I didn't see them making love. It was mostly just feeling. I had to make them age appropriate in the dream. I mean the lovers, Cindy and Willy. Because they are both teenagers. Yea, that's why I think it's an Oedipus thing, or the jealousy thing, or both. Many meanings. Shit, you know that!

I carry social taboos into my unconscious. I've always

done that. Even into my daydreams. My conscious fantasies. My wakeful fantasies. It drives me crazy. I hate that.
Sure, I'm inhibited, even in my fantasies. I've known that.
Didn't I ever tell you that? Oh, yea. I usually get hung-up
at the point of what I am wearing. I knew one other person
. . . I don't usually discuss this with people, but I happened
to mention it once to Connie. Connie was my friend from
New York that I told you about. She said the same thing
used to happen to her. She used to get hung-up on what
she was wearing. If you're going to fantasize that you're
coming into a room, and everyone stops dead and stares
at you 'cause you're terrific and fantastic, you get hung-up
on what you're wearing. And you never get into the room.

It was awful. I never could control it. That's why whenever Jeff said you're the director of your dreams, I thought,
that's a crock of shit, I'm not. I'm not even the director of
my fantasies. Connie's really funny. I haven't written to
anybody in a long time. And . . . uhm, I'm beginning to get
the guilts about it, but not so much that I'm gonna sit down
and write. And I got a note from Connie. I hadn't written
to her, I guess, since way before Christmas. She writes very
short little notes and drops bombs in them. Her last letter
said,

> I've really been worried about you. What's
> happening? How come I haven't heard from
> you? I'd call you, but Steve's out of a job. . . .

Now Steve was a junky, for like twenty years. They have
been out of Synanon for—I don't know how long it is—
about five or six months. Yea, about six months. And they
have a baby that will be about a year old. Anyway . . .
so . . .

> Steve's out of a job, and I can't call you. I got
> pregnant. The IUD slipped, and Steve made me
> get an abortion, and I hated the whole thing. I

130

was really angry with him. Never again. When I got home, I started to bleed and had to go back into the hospital, where I got seventeen pints of blood transfused. Now they think I have serum hepatitis. The baby is fully recovered from the brain concussion. Life is very happy, and bla, bla, bla. Please write.

Love,
Connie

And she's always done that. It's just terrific. She's just wild. So I . . . uhm, then I got another letter from our friend, Judy, the witch. I've mentioned Myrna, right? My best friend who died of a malignant melanoma, and I gave her my favorite . . . it was her favorite, too . . . my favorite painting the day before she died. Well, Judy and Roger were Myrna's dearest friends for many years. It was with them that she lived her last months of life.

And then a year later, Roger died. He died shortly before we moved here. Judy has got three teenage kids, and Judy is like nobody else in the whole world. She's incredible. She's a yogi. And she's a witch. And she's a bitch. And she's very masculine. And she's very womanly. And she's just a ton of bricks. She's just wild. A most amazing mother. She does really wild, crazy things like writing to the governor and getting arrested for protesting in the nude. She's into the creative, and having visions, and painting bones on her car. Oh, she's just wild. Really a neat lady. See, I'm put in charge of the Martians by her, because Jeff and Gil are the Martians. And she figures that by now their antennae have tangled. She . . . it just goes on and on like this. But in many ways, Judy's in our world. Oh, in many cases, yea. Right up to her neck. Because she's always worked. Roger was a writer, and in that sense, their roles were switched. Every once in a while, he made some money on it. Usually not. Roger was the gentle, kind one. It was really an interesting thing. Judy was always the tough

131

. . . what . . . like a non-Jewish, Golda Meir. So that's Judy. Except she's also into mysticals. I don't think Golda Meir was into mysticals.

Judy is the kind of lady . . . her daughter, little Myrna, who's named after our friend Myrna . . . uhm . . . was in one of those awful accidents when she was young. She's about fifteen or sixteen now. She was in one of those awful comas out of which she was supposed to come a vegetable, if she comes at all. And Judy and Roger didn't buy that. For six weeks or two months or whatever it was, they went to the hospital every day. They talked to her and read to her and moved her arms and legs so they wouldn't get stiff. And Myrna came out of it, and they brought her through her infancy again, at age nine or so, and the whole thing. And now the kid's working and going to group therapy at a free clinic and writing a musical play. She wrote to me, too, in the letter with Judy. It was really wild. Wild, doc. . . . Almost like a dream.

Thirteen

THE CYRANO SYNDROME

HERE I AM ON THIS COUCH AGAIN. It's like I never leave this place. There isn't anything to talk about. I've talked about the women in the *group*, and Jeff and Cindy, and Connie and Judy and Roger and Hercules and a dozen others. So there's nothing to talk about except . . . me. I haven't talked about me in a really long time. Most of the time I'm just bored. Most of my life is boring. Nothing more to say. That's all. It's nobody's fault. I like to pretend it's other people's fault because that's easier. It's not. It's my fault, doc. It's all just a big bore. People who are bored don't have enthusiasm and humor and feel. Which is what I don't have. At least not now.

I poured out some creative energy with Gil today, keeping him alive in the doctor's office. It takes a lot out of me doing that. So I played good mother. That's terrific. I mean I think it's important. I hope it will hold him in good stead when he's older and says, buzz-off, Mom. I come through for Gil when he's scared. We laugh and we giggle. We were there for an hour-and-a-half until this woman comes in finally and looks in his ears. And all the while, he knew he was gonna get a shot. I knew he probably wouldn't. We joked. We fooled around. We played tic-tac-toe. We rapped. I don't rap to him like he's a kid. I rap to him like he's Gil. Because that's who he is.

But then I'm exhausted after. It was fun. But after, I'm pooped. After, I want something else. And there isn't anything else in my life. And Cindy's leaving, so that's another zero. One time I blurted out in here that I didn't

133

want to get sucked up into Jeffy's . . . his bag of evils, his bag of demons. I got enough of my own. Well, I still feel that way. I think the thing that bugs me, especially like when I had that dream about a week ago about Willy, is the feeling that I have of being sexually attracted to somebody. Wanting somebody.

I don't feel that way about Jeff. Very seldom in recent times, if ever. And I find that very sad. And boring. Maybe Jeff feels the same way, too. I don't know. It isn't easy for me to share these sad feelings with you. Share! I hate that stupid word! It's not easy for me to dump that kind of stuff here. Or anywhere. Easier here than in the *group,* but, nevertheless, difficult here as well. Great. You're a pro. Maybe it's easier to tell it if I say I dump than if I say I share. I suppose I'm not supposed to feel that way. I don't know.

What am I supposed to do with it? I don't know if it's his bag or my bag or what. I only know I don't enjoy screwing with him. And I don't think he enjoys screwing with me. First of all, he doesn't get enough, in terms of quantity. And I don't get enough in quality. So, maybe he doesn't get quality, either. There you are. And it drives him up the wall that I won't spread my legs at the snap of his finger, or be available for grabbing of tit, grabbing of ass all the time. I mean I can't even bend over without getting a finger up my ass. I don't dig it. Sure, I've gone through all the conversation of, Jeff stop treating me like a table or a chair.

So I get a bunch of women's lib garbage back in my face. I mean I used to feel that way before women's libers started rapping. So what! Like I said, I don't know what he feels about the quality. I know he doesn't like it when I'm overweight, except I have bigger tits. He did find . . . I knew he always felt that way. I knew that was one of the reasons he hadn't bugged me more about being fat, because he hates me being fat. He finally said it the other day. He said the reason I probably don't kick you out when you're

134

fat is because you got big tits when you're fat. He's a big tit man. Terrific. I'm thrilled to death for him.

I tell him they are my tits and not his, no matter how much he wants to think about it the other way around. But he doesn't agree with that. No. Of course not. He thinks I'm a selfish bitch. He loves me. He needs me. All of those things are true, too, but he also thinks I'm a selfish bitch. With fat and big tits. . . . That my goal in life ought to be the family unit, he tells me. It drives me up the wall. In our household—now this is excluding Cindy, but she's been right in the mold, too, while she's been here—there are three or four individuals. Five counting the stupid dog. And it is not a family unit like you see on TV. It just isn't. We are much more like the Cohens in that sense. Thank God I lived with them. So I know somebody else lived this way. My own family was that way. There isn't such a thing as a family unit. I mean, if there is, I haven't experienced it. We all dig each other. But, God, we are volatile individuals. Clashing. Competing with each other. All the time. It makes him crazy.

I don't know what to do about it. He thinks I'm selfish. He thinks I come to therapy in order to brush away whatever hang-ups and cobwebs I got, so I can go out and be a famous painter, or a famous writer. He thinks I still have those old fantasies. That's why I'm coming to therapy! It's funny. To me, I don't know. It's just really funny. We are two people who are constantly living this side of suicidal thoughts. Sometimes that side.

Competing. Who's the most suicidal. It's really weird. It's stupid. It's dumb. It's wasteful. It's meaningless. It's boring. And what does Jeff give to the family unit concept? Well, you want to know from my point of view? Nothing. And when I have indicated such, I have gotten a big blast. So I don't say too much. Jeff thinks that way 'cause he's out busting his ass, you know. He'd rather be sitting on the beach, so he says. And that I am a stupid and dumb bitch for always thinking, all these years, that . . . uhm. . . .

It never occurred to me that this man wasn't going to earn a good living. It always occurred to him that he wasn't. And I just learned that. I finally said, well, what do you want from me? What if I'd been the other kind of woman? What if I would say, yea, yea, I'm frightened, everytime you went into your paranoid rampage, that failure-is-just-around-the-corner? From the time he left C.C.N.Y. up until now, he kept telling me, oh, God, tomorrow we're going on welfare.

What if I would switch and say, that's right. What are we gonna do? How are we gonna pay the bills? Uhm, then he'd say, that's irrelevant. You can't talk to me. You can't communicate with me. Which is true. There are times when things are neat with us. So, you know, if I keep my big mouth shut, things are fine. If I don't, if I get on my defensive hobbyhorse, then things are not fine. He gets super paranoid. I don't know. I don't know what he means by family unit. I really don't know. He raps about it all the time. When I make suggestions . . . I say, okay, let's . . . I suppose whenever I think of doing things together, it means like going someplace, 'cause I'm always wanting to go someplace. We don't go anywhere! Family, or not family.

It's just really quite the opposite from what some of the ladies were saying in the *group*. This man, unlike their husbands, wants to be home. They can't get their husbands home, and I can't get Jeffy out. This man hates it out there, in the outside world. You know, it's incredible. I don't know if you saw it. *The Producers* was on TV. I've been wanting to see *The Producers* since it first came out. And, uhm . . . this is really funny. Jeff is in there watching and laughing away. I said, why didn't you tell me about this? My head is filled with trivia. I just know who wrote it, who's married to whom. I just know all that Hollywood shit. It just sticks in my head like glue. It's a family joke. Anyway, he didn't tell me it was on.

You know, he's so caught up in his own troubles . . . uhm . . . reading the newspaper ain't gonna get him out of the doldrums. But maybe seeing a decent flick where there's some creativity in there, maybe reading a book other than *Crime In America*, maybe going to the theater, maybe that would provide some kind of entertainment. Anything! It doesn't even have to be very esoteric. But, no. Taking a ride to look at the leaves in the autumn . . . forget that. Jeff tells me, I drive in that goddamn car everyday down Route 95—you try it someday, he says.

Okay, well, I can't try it. Because I'm just as much to blame. I'm not woman's liber who wants to go out and make a big career in the big beautiful world. I hate the stupid world, too. I don't want to get paid for doing a lot of shit. There's not a creative job out there. I'm scared out there. I don't like it. And God knows, even if I went out there, I certainly couldn't bring in the kind of bread he does. You know, so we can take our kid every week for allergy shots and twice a week so we can have them listen . . . listen to his lungs. And that will go on for the next five years. So I don't know about the family unit. The family unit, it is . . . I don't know. He talks about making . . . he said . . . I guess we're gonna try to buy a house, maybe in the summer. A house is supposed to make a family unit. Beautiful. He keeps saying he doesn't need people. That he doesn't need friends. Okay, terrific. But I can't be everything to him. And he can't be everything to me. Maybe for him, this mysterious family unit is the answer. Not so for me.

I really am. . . . I'm always feeling alienated in that *group*. One, because I'm not a Catholic. And, now, suddenly I feel alienated because the hassles Jeff and I have are probably hassles, which if I ever blurted them out, the ladies would say, God, my husband's never home. Your husband's always there. What are you bitching about? The grass is greener and all that shit, I guess.

I mean underneath all this garbage, there's good stuff. It's true. We got a lot of good stuff. But I don't know . . . this . . . this experience with therapy is so different for me that I don't know how to judge it. I know it drives him crazy. It makes him upset. He figures it's all a bunch of crap. Because it doesn't make me a better piece of ass! When I went to Rosenberg, for whatever happened there, I was better in bed. Or at least I would ball more often, or it was of more quality, or I was opening up, or was freer, or bla, bla, bla, bla, bla. You know, all of that. It was terrific. It was nice. But temporary. Still it was nice at the time, doc.

I mean having orgasms is better than not. Feeling turned-on is better than not. I don't care if it lasts only two or three weeks, or three years. What was right for me back then isn't right for me now. I'm just saying that was what happened to me in that experience. That's how I used to use therapy. Well, I'm not being allowed by you to use therapy for those reasons any more, I guess. Why do I accept Jeff's shit and anger for his being out in the world? As I tell you, Jeff tells me the world is only bad. He just hates it out there. You dig it? Like Route 95 is out to kill him.

Whenever any of the ladies in the *group* say anything about Jeff that borders on the derogatory, even if they comment to clarify something that I am angry at him for, I realized recently that I automatically spring to his defense. Yea, like it's okay if I say my nose is big, but it's not okay if you say I have a big nose. I can cut him down, but they can't. That's what I call the Cyrano Syndrome. Like Cyrano de Bergerac.

This man says a lot of things to me, most of which he doesn't hear, and someday I'm gonna tape it and play it back to him. From time to time, he calls me a fantastic intellectual, Jew bitch, parasite, fat pig. . . . Usually not at the same time, like I'm telling you now. But often in the same week. Or within the same time span that's within my head. As I'm hearing the bong echoes of the one, I'm suddenly getting the counterpoint of the other. There may have been quite a few days in between, to be factual. I have to accept that Jeff can feel all of these things. A gambit

138

about me, because I know that I feel all of those things about him. Not that he's a parasite, but from positive to negative charges that I feel going back and forth. The love him, hate him routine.

That's why I don't like to talk about my painting with him. If I refer to the money as your money, he hates it. He hates it when I get into these pronouns, as he calls them. Well, I do that because he calls me a parasite. He says, you haven't contributed—look at all these women who can make three hundred or six hundred a month by calling and soliciting on the phone, right? Well, marvelous. Terrific. The three years that I worked, the year that we lived together that I used my bank account to help him pay the rent; that doesn't count. He only remembers the fifty cents I wouldn't pay him the first breakfast we had together. 'Cause I'd been giving out money and all to a bunch of shit-heads who never gave it back to me. And that fifty cents was about the last straw. It's a funny joke. It's not a joke.

That happened . . . see, Jeffy and I . . . we . . . I met him and then we went out. And I guess the first night we slept together, whatever . . . the next morning, we went to breakfast. I'd been working at this hot dog stand, going around with a lot of beatnik kids who didn't have any money, and I was always shelling out money. Not a lot. I had about five hundred bucks in a bank account. And I was earning some cash on the side, working at the hot dog stand when I was living at the Cohens.

So, the first breakfast, he was fifty cents short. He said to me, you got fifty cents to pay for the breakfast? And I said, I don't wanna give you fifty cents, or whatever I said. And he's never forgotten it. Well, thereafter, when we lived together, except I was still at the Cohens, but whenever I wasn't needed there, I was at his place. And we opened up a joint bank account. We pooled whatever money we had. He was on a fellowship getting three hundred dollars a month, and he was into therapy three times a week, and paying sixty dollars a month for an apartment, and I was working at the hot dog stand, selling hot dogs for four bits. And I was living at the Cohens. And I had this account from the years that I had worked, since I was in high school. So, we pooled our money.

It was our money, then, right? And all the time I was working, it was our money. But since I quit working, and since there's the hassle, the constant hassle about the goddamn shrink, I decided to call it his money. The fact that I take care of our kid . . . okay, so I'm not the greatest domestic in the world. That used to be a badge-of-honor. He was kind of thrilled that his wife wasn't the domestic. I was the social worker. I mean, he is kind of a man's woman's liber in that sense. And he was before. I guess maybe I just don't do any of the stuff . . . uhm . . . really terrific or without bitching. I bitch about it. I don't like to pick up dog shit. I didn't like to pick up Gilly's shit, either. I am really thrilled that Gil is a person now—and not just an ass-hole.

I mean, is that bad? I don't know. I guess it's bad to bitch. Old Mr. Stoic never bitches. He can sit on his sore hemorrhoids driving seven hundred miles across country and never say a word about his ass. He'll scream at me for not being able to read a map, but not a word about his hemorrhoids. Well, terrific. I ain't made that way. See, a lot of this stuff . . . this is not stuff I hold in. It comes out in our dialogues from time to time, and it comes out in just this very ugly, crappy way with nothing happening at the end.

Feeling this way, I find it very difficult to be turned on and excited about making love. In the first place, it's usually done in the morning when I'm half asleep, and I don't even see the head of my partner. His head is over there somewhere. Over there. Side fucking. It's really intimate. It is so intimate that I usually wind up stifling screams. 'Cause I couldn't really say that side fucking in the morning, when I'm half asleep and can't even see his

140

goddamn head, is exactly pleasant. Jeff should know that. I don't know if he knows how I feel. Yea, he knows. I don't know, maybe he doesn't know. Maybe he doesn't even care. I don't know if he knows or not. Hey, I just did the Cyrano again. This time I even did it to myself.

I'd like to ask the bastard. But it would be really hard to do. What am I gonna say, look here, Jeff, I don't like to fuck that way. Then you know what he's gonna say? He's gonna say, you don't like to fuck any way. And if you want to know the truth, that's true. I really don't, recently. Except on my terms. And if that's bad, unwomanly, Jew-bitch, rotten parasite, then I don't give a shit. Goddamn right.

Maybe I'll just ask . . . tell him what I feel. Uhm . . . what am I gonna say? I can't tell him, you don't turn me on anymore. He'll just say, great, you can go back to New York with your niece. But don't take my son with you. That's what he will say. That's what he always says, go back with your goddamn Jewish family, but you're not taking my son.

And you know what I hear underneath all of that? I hear him say, Pam, why are we killing each other? We love each other so fucking much. God, why do we do this to each other? Must be a faulty gene. Bad environment. Unprogressive school education. There must be some reason for it. I must get into these sexual feelings, doc. Their absence for Jeff, that is. Maybe next time. Better get a sponge for your couch. Your next patient will think there is a leak in the roof. I came in here feeling nice and neutral and bored. And I leave soaking wet. Maybe I'll catch pneumonia. Can rotten parasites catch pneumonia, doc?

FOURTEEN

A NAUGHTY ORGASM

THIRTY-THREE YEARS OLD, and I'm still with sexual hang-ups. I can't believe it, but it's true. Jeffy and I had a sexual encounter I feel I've got to talk to you about. It's hard to talk to you about these things. Rosenberg, he was just a fat old man. It was a little different. But uhm . . . there are times when I'm not sure . . . Jeffy said to me . . . oh, I don't know, some shit on TV, . . . and he said I'm not always a good lay, meaning him. Well, I didn't answer his question. I just said, well, neither am I. Sometimes I'm great, sometimes I stink. He said, no, you're always great. So that leaves me up the wall, right? Nothing I can say then. But what I said was, neah, I don't believe that. And I just sort of let it hang there. Really awful. Maybe that's the castrating part of me. My laughing now must be because . . . it's so private. It's not funny. It's really difficult.

So, there we were one night—fucking—she said to herself, and uhm . . . I don't know whether I'm particularly thinking of giving. I am thinking of getting, and I don't want to get hung-up. A lot of times I get hung-up. Uhm, so. . . .

I thought Jeff had come. It was only hours later . . . I mean not hours when I . . . but about an hour later I realized he hadn't, though he'd told me he had had an orgasm. Maybe he did, but didn't come. Ejaculate. I don't know about men's physiology, and I can't seem to read Masters and Johnson. And I sort of had a clitoral thing. One of those . . . uhm. . . . I'm borrowing a word from Rosenberg because I don't know that much about it myself . . . he

143

called it a fractured thing. That you want to go on and have more. But it's better to have this half thing than nothing at all. And he got really angry. I guess I don't like to talk when I'm screwing. I . . . I. . . . It distracts . . . I just don't dig it. On occasion he's asked me to talk, or he'll talk, and he'll say . . . ask me different things. I don't like that. Uhm . . . but I, it throws . . . I don't like it. But sometimes I will scream out something like —suck me. And, wham, he got really angry. He says it's either on my terms or your terms. No, first I guess what he said was, it always has to be on your terms. These are phrases that he's used. Sprinkled throughout our life from time to time. I suppose a little bit more in recent years. And I said, what the hell's the matter with you? You had your orgasm, didn't you? He said, yea. And I said, well, I had something, so what's bugging you?

I think he wasn't at this point . . . I think he said something that indicated he wasn't just saying I only want it on my terms. But this kind of battle was going on. His terms, my terms . . . all of this. And I said, oh, shit, you don't know . . . something like you don't know anything about what a woman feels. And he yells, oh, come on! I said, well, you don't know anything about what I feel. I didn't really care if he was pissed. I usually get kind of devastated. My usual thing. I feel the guilts and the whole crap. I didn't let him play a tune on me this time. I argued back and I didn't feel bad.

See, I still do get the scaries. 'Cause my sexual experience was so crappy before I started sleeping with Jeff. Have I ever talked about it? Is it important? Oh, god, it will take forever.

There weren't very many guys. But most of it . . . I can sum it up 'cause I've talked a lot about it in therapy before. I wasn't really interested in making love with anybody. Having sex with anybody. I was just so damn sick of saying no. And I was so damn sick of the shit my mother had put in my head. See, I was so up-tight that I could barely,

144

you know, spread the legs. Truly. I actually was too scared to spread the legs. And there were guys, because of this, that told me that I was physically deformed. And all that crap. And most of it was from enormously horney guys who'd come on my knees before they'd even enter me. Yet I still believed them, and I . . . at least partly believed that I was physically deformed.

What the hell did I know? I didn't know from shit. I was lucky I never got knocked up. I mean sperms crawling up my thighs. It's funny I suppose. Once in a while the penis got inside. There was only one decent time. It happened to be with a guy . . . uhm, this guy Scott, . . . this all becomes very incestuous as things tended to do in and around C.C.N.Y. in those days. Uhm, I was dating this guy Scotty, and I never had an orgasm. Didn't even know what the hell it was. Read about . . . you get pink all over and see stars, bla, bla, bla. And one night at his place, I'd suddenly realized that's what I'd had. I didn't feel up-tight. I felt good. It was fantastic.

I didn't like Scotty much at that point, so it was peculiar that it happened then. I was cooling off on him. He wasn't the first I screwed with. But the one I first experienced orgasm with, even though I was cooling off on him. And he was the last guy before Jeff. There might have been six guys, I suppose. The first guy I screwed with is a whole 'nother story. I don't have time for Ivanoff today. He was impotent. I thought it a funny joke at the time considering I finally said yes to him, and he goes—phffft—soft. So it was really funny. He used to masturbate a lot. That was a sick scene in my life. Terrible. Terrible bad dream. Really mucked me up. Almost as much as my mother.

I was on a date with Scotty at a party the night I met Jeff. Did I ever tell you how we met? Went to this party. I was cool on Scotty. He was making me sick. I used to go roll dog food into pellets for his rats—he was a psychologist. You know, rats in their maze. Well, I used to make their pellets. Anyway, I went to this party, and there were

145

a bunch of people in the psych program at C.C.N.Y. It was the summer before I was a senior, and in walked these three guys. Allen Wilson, and another guy, Mark, who wound up at Binghamton State Hospital, and Jeff. My immediate thought was, oh, it's Saturday night, and in walked these three guys—they must be queer. I'd heard about Allen, who was like six-feet-four. It had to do with a tape I heard of Allen's laugh. He had one of those crazy kind of laughs. UGGGH, UGGGH, that booms out over the stadium. So I was sort of trying to see what was happening with Allen. Well, that was the night we discussed the possibility of assassinating Franco. That's why, when I hear about the Berrigans, I think it's all so funny.

And I was interested in Jeff. I thought he sort of looked like Jack Paar. In any case, I wanted to go swimming. Scotty had a cold and didn't want to go swimming, but he drove me back home to get my bathing suit. Home is . . . I was still living at the Cohens. I came back to the party, and I said, who's gonna go swimming with me? It was at an apartment building. And Jeff said, I would, except I don't have a bathing suit, and I don't wear underwear. And that was intriguing. I'd been going with a lot of schleps up until then. A lot of guys slobbering on me, telling me what terrific potential I had. So the host gave Jeff a bathing suit, and we went to the pool. And the lights were on, and I was swimming around trying to be as sexy as I knew how to be, and Allen Wilson comes out on the cat walk above, and he says something down to me like, this guy's been very disillusioned by women, and he needs a woman to do something for him, blablabla. So I'm swimming around and not a touch. Nothing. And Jeff . . . aaah, he's such a cool character, he starts telling me about this graph that he had on women. First of all, he said, women don't stimulate him anymore, and I'm biting at this worm, this hook. Ha. He has this graph on women with intelligence, lust level, grades in school, boob size, and so on. He had ten women, and he was grading them on this graph, which he used to predict how good they would be in bed as the unknown.

I thought it was terrific. This cool, cool, aloof guy who hadn't made one single pass at me and was very romantic. And we get out and start toweling-off and, you know, started walking up to the party. And he puts his hand on my back, real sexy like, and he says, if it's important to you to see me again, you'll get me the necessary information. So I go in and quickly get dressed and I lean over to my date, Scotty, who's pissed by this time, and I say, gimme a pencil. He said, what are you doing? I said, I'm writing my name and address down for that guy over there. And I gave it to Allen to give to Jeff, and Scotty said, let's go home. And we went home.

Later, Scotty married the girl that Jeff had recently stopped living with just before he met me. It was all very . . . like this. Two weeks later the son-of-a-bitch calls me. He says, I was going through my suit to send it to the cleaners and I found your address, would you like to go out? And I said, sure. So I took him out to the Circle, which was a little restaurant on the Island. Then I took him to my favorite beach spot. I don't know what possessed me. I must have fallen in love with the guy. It was great. From then on we lived together.

I was still at the Cohens, but any time they didn't need me, I lived at his place for the rest of my senior year. Terrible. It was on Saturday mornings when I had my shrink appointment at student health. I used to fall out of bed and run to the shrink with half my buttons unbuttoned. You know in those days we didn't wear bras either, but it wasn't a big political thing. It was just more comfortable. I remember once climbing up a muddy hill to get to the shrink. Muddied up his goddamn couch. Looked like Hercules had shit on it. It was such a funny scene. I don't know why I'm laughing at all of this. But that was almost twelve years ago when we met. Oh . . . but to tie it up to the orgasm with Scotty. . . .

147

See, Scotty started going with the girl who had lived with Jeff. This girl was an enormously bright woman. Very, very bright woman. I say was because several years ago she committed suicide. I hated her guts. I still hate even the memory of her. I was so envious . . . she was the only woman I've ever known . . . personally known who was sexually confident. She just . . . she wasn't any great beauty or anything. She was just sexually confident. And I had so many hang-ups. Oh, god. I was just in awe of this person. She was in student health, too, at the time, with some other shrink. Anyway, she . . . this was early on, when Jeff and I were first going together . . . Jeff and I had lunch together at school. And he said. . . .

He said, I was talking to Rita today, that was her name, and she told me that Scotty told her that he gave you your first orgasm. And, uhm . . . my response to that was—isn't it a nice day. Which Kaplin, my shrink at the time, didn't think was the appropriate response. So it was like . . . I figured out that . . . how certain groups of people value virginity. And husbands get really wiped out if they think some other guy took the virginity or broke the hymen of their wife. This orgasm deal was just one step away. Jeff didn't care about virginity, but he did care about that orgasm. I don't want to get into my philosophical views about this.

Let me wind up today with Ivanoff, the impotent. Actually Ivanoff, the perverter. I've only got ten minutes left, and Ivanoff was a whole year of my life, so maybe I can just hit the highlights. I was a sophomore. I'd left the dormitory and I'd found a place to live. I moved in with a young couple, Herbert and Marla Gross. Herbert's father owned a big art store, and Herbie was running the place. He was so rich I couldn't conceive of it. They just built this seven bedroom house with ten foot doors and a living room that nobody ever went into. Indoor swimming pool and all. And they had two little adopted girls and then they finally had their own third daughter, who was the ugliest, horriblest little kid. And I told Marla, yea, I know all about little kids 'cause, see, I was supposed to help out. That's why they let me move in there. To be mother's helper.

I was very lonely. I didn't . . . as is my thing . . . I didn't . . . see, I wasn't dating, and I just cut myself off from my friends in the dormitory. Herbie fixed me up with this fraternity schmuck. I think he was the son of one of the three stooges. It was a horrendous time.

Anyway, I met Ivanoff standing in line registering for a physical-ed class. Ivanoff was originally Rumanian, I think. It was difficult to piece together— what was true about Ivanoff. This was what, 1957? After the Hungarian thing. So he was a Hungarian refugee. He fought against the Soviet Union in the great revolution that fell apart. If he ever went back, they'd kill him. He'd been in prison, and on and on. He was kind of short, like me. Short with dark hair and kind of stubby. But marvelous eyes. Uhm . . . I haven't thought about Ivanoff in detail in a long time. Anyway I had not . . . had I . . . no, I had not . . . I had barely petted with anybody until the time I met Ivanoff. I never even masturbated, if you can believe that. So Ivanoff introduced me to all these lovely things.

He masturbated all the time. All the time! Anywhere! Everywhere! It was incredible. I mean anywhere. When he was driving with me in the car; when we'd be studying; when he was eating a meal; in a movie; at times even in class; once in a telephone booth. He also was living in a kind of mother's helper situation. He talked about . . . you have to understand how green I was. I didn't know from anything about anything. You know, I was a little sophomore philosophy major running around in her Bermuda shorts.

He talked about perversions, and he loved the Marquis de Sade and this garbage. I had zillions of letters from him, which I burned one summer lest my mother would find them when I brought all my stuff home. His letters had all his fantasies of my pissing on him and shitting on him, and putting objects in his rectum. All of that kind of garbage.

149

He introduced me to oral sex. He kept saying, probably because he was impotent, that . . . he would go like this. . . . This is just, uhh . . . I can't remember the words he used. He had this thick accent. But to him conventional sexual intercourse was . . . pwttt . . . child's play. Nothing. Cunnilingus and fellatio and all these other things, even devices, that was where it was at, though we didn't use those phrases in those days. Well, uhm . . . I thought I was living in some novel. It was terrific.

It was also very scarey. He was living at one point; he'd gotten this place to stay . . . it was like a castle, this house. Up in Westchester County somewhere, where the millionaires lived. There was a room with two huge grand pianos that this couple played. I don't remember their names. It was an enormous estate. It was like out of Sherlock Holmes. I think it was that night. I was lying on top of him, and he . . . I don't know how he asked me . . . but he asked me to fuck or something. In my head, I just said, yes. I always had my mother's face in my head; just push her away and quit saying no. All that crap. So I said, yes. And the guy couldn't do it. Remember I was into philosophy, and existentialism at the time, and the theater of the absurd. The word absurd was all around in these young intellectual circles. So funny. And I thought, of course, Pammie, it's part of the absurd universe.

I mean, I didn't really feel bad. I suppose in some sense I was sort of relieved, because I was sort of scared. I didn't even think of birth control. It didn't even enter my mind. I must've thought I was some sort of saint that I wouldn't get pregnant. But I just thought it was funny that when I finally said yes, nothing happened. I remember . . . how old was I, twenty-one? I remember this guy always masturbating and talking about masturbating. So I went home, and I masturbated with a little fluffy dog animal that I had. And I had an orgasm. It was the first, you know clitoral orgasm. It was the first time I ever experienced that. And you know what my thought was? I never told anybody

150

this. Not even all my other shrinks. My thought was—what the hell do I need men for? That was my first thought.

I've always regretted having that thought. That was a bad bit of business. Howsomever . . . one time though, he tried . . . we were at the Gross', and nobody was home. I've got to cut this short. It goes on forever. He tried to make me in . . . they had a den on the lower level with huge solid glass windows that faced right smack onto the street. They had tinted glass and no curtains. And he tried to make me there in Herbert's and Marla's house, and I'm screaming. Hollering. He was shoving me around and ripping off my clothes. And this went on for ten minutes. And then he left and said this was the end. He took off in his car, and I panicked. I just panicked and what I did was . . . Marla was away with the kids at the time, and it must have been a Sunday, that's right. And I ran all the way down, several blocks, to the art store. Herbie was in there doing inventory or something.

Crying. Sobbing. Everything. Banging on the door. And poured my heart out to Herbie, that I hadn't given myself, and everything that had happened. I told Herbert I still loved Ivanoff; please help me find him. Can you imagine, I thought I loved him? Oh, my god, as I think about it, it's like another person. Yea, I thought I loved the man. I thought he was terrific. All this stuff.

At one point, we said we were gonna get married. My parents only vaguely knew that I was dating this guy. But see, then I got Herbert into my life, which was the worst possible thing in the whole wide world to do. Herbie loved manipulating people's lives, and there I was on sobbing knees, please help me.

I remember I said to Ivanoff, let's tell my parents, and he said, oh, no, we're going to go to California and get married —your parents have nothing to do with us. Well, then suddenly my senses came back. My good middle class, bourgeois background saved me from this insane man. I cut it off. And I couldn't live at the Gross' anymore, so that at the end of that school year I just cut out and went home for the summer. And I decided I'd look for a new place to live the following year, because Herbert had gotten too involved in my life. I just sat home and listened to records all summer. I didn't even work. The only thing I did all summer was to find a place . . . a family to live with in the fall.

The funny thing was, when I came back to school to live at the Cohen's, the first time I saw Ivanoff on campus, I was just panicked. There was a scene once with a knife at my throat that I ought to tell you about when there's time. I kept my cool. It was sort of interesting. He could have slit my throat, I suppose. The man was insane.

There was a course on campus taught by a Dominican Monk on dialectical materialism, and all the communists and Bolsheviks and socialists were in this course. And Ivanoff was running about with these guys. Later I started going around with these people, and they said they'd make a socialist out of me. And I said, no, I don't give a shit about any of that. They had introduced Ivanoff to all the communist party members and whatever the hell they were doing off campus. Well, I told the communists he was a Hungarian refugee, and they sent him a note saying they'd kill him if he ever went to another of their meetings. Everyone was scared out of their pants. Really funny.

I gotta blast out of here. I'm overtime, I know.

FIFTEEN

THE LONDON FOG

WHAT HAVE YOU DONE? What is that? A fancy new chair. Yea. Oh, that's just like our sofa. I mean our whole sofa is gold fuzzy, just like your new chair. You expecting somebody? Getting all these chairs in here. You're Mr. Furry living in your fuzzy chair. That's neat. That's really neat. Something to wake up the patients.

How am I, doc? Tell me quick, before you say, *you tell me.* It's a good day today. It's pretty out. Sun is shining. Remember that analogy you told me, sometime ago, about the ropes? You talked about me using them to climb the mountain and all the while I'd be getting better. Well, I had rope burns on my hands, after the *group* Tuesday, holding on to those ropes. And I was really glad you were there with the ropes. That was a weird session for me. I can't remember exactly what it was that was so scarey. My blockers are working fast and furious. I don't know quite what to make of it all. There was just so much coming out and so much coming in. Lots was happening all at once. It seems like Grace really got through to me, by saying that whatever she would say wouldn't get through. And something Noreen said when I asked her how it was going with her and her husband. She said something to the effect that . . . things change but. . . . Well, I have to go on to my own words, because whatever she said made me think that you can't calculate and plan change. You just wake up one day, and it's changed. I'm thinking of change for the better, since she said things were better for her since starting therapy. Better for me, too, somehow.

It was hard for me not to—I'm not sure I was successful —not to respond with guilts vis-a-vis Helen, when she walked out in the middle of the *group* session. Because I didn't . . . the week before and this week, I'm . . . it seemed very difficult for her. And it's easy for me to grasp onto the guilts in that kind of scene. I thought something I said caused her to leave. That's why I shut up. Margaret responded in her same old way. I suppose the hardest time for me was when everybody was really quiet. Nine women sitting in deafening, loud silence. In the quiet. I thought, how come all of you don't blast me? That was so hard to say. I didn't know what to do with the silence. The anxiety really gets to me in the quiet. Do all your patients in *groups* find the silence so hard to handle?

I'm not sure I know what to do when they say something either, but at least it's something I can chew on. I can't chew on the silence. I needed to hear Helen call me a dope. And when she said, it isn't a bunch of crap that you tell us, just say it, and stop all your filtering. Stop all the worrying about what we will think of you if you're only talking crap; it's real what you're saying and you're not the only one that's been there. Something like that. Really nice. I could feel she liked me even though she was angry; maybe because she was angry. You don't waste angries on people you don't care about. I needed to hear that because I'm . . . the day before, and the days before that, I was ready to chuck those beliefs about what makes me crazy about Jeff. So I'm in a silence. . . . In a way, it's kind of paradoxical since I opened up some. But I've been in more than one sort of silence recently. I haven't written to anybody for months. It's not right not to write to people you love. To friends. Silence in the *group* brings outside silence into sharp focus. I continue the same old pattern of cutting myself off from people. Even if they are far away.

I have that thing. I've always had that thing of—absence is more real than presence. Emptiness is more real than fullness. It's just like when I'm with somebody, and I know

I'm not going to be with that person forever. Sometimes I try to make it really count. But I'm always surrounded by the coming absence. The coming going away of the person. And when they go away, that's more real. That's always been there anyway. And then, when it is an actual fact, it's just more real to me than when they are there. The feeling of the space. The feeling of . . . I don't know how to put it. My experiencing it is something I don't describe very well.

I'm not sure if I spelled it out in the *group* on Tuesday about Jeff's and my crazies being the same. That is such a nebulous word. Our competition, our needs are very much the same. If, from my point of view, if . . . uhm . . . I feel that he doesn't want to share me with other people. It's also true that I feel the same way about him. So that if I only describe one of us, him or me, it's wrong. I don't think I did all of it . . . how I felt that he wasn't empathic or sympathetic or didn't lend his sensitivities to how I felt about Cindy's leaving, because it takes me away from him. What are you so sympathetic with that little chick for? I'm bleeding here, he says to me. In the opposite way, I do the same thing when he comes home and cries about the people of Chile, or the people of Peru. I remember writing it once in a letter that I did not mail, saying I couldn't care if the people of Chile just dropped off into the Pacific. I meant it. I was in competition with the people of Chile for his tears, his feeling. And we do this to each other, and it's really bad.

The part where he's jealous of what my feelings are for somebody else is stronger when it concerns somebody from my family, I think. Much more so. Much more so. Then, in my raps with Cindy, I'm in the same position as I've always been with anybody. The same position of explaining Jeff to whoever they are. And I'm tired of that. And see, then I have to explain them to him, too. And I'm also tired of that. He saw Cindy as a young . . . mostly, until toward the end of her stay with us . . . mostly as a gal who's grown up with the same shit as every woman who grows up in my family has. That is to say, she puts down men. Except me. He says I'm the exception. But often he doesn't act like that's what he thinks. Jeff sees it in me from time to time.

He battles it. He knows very well that I've battled it all my life as well. But he saw her as showing no respect. That men are nothing and on and on. It was the same old story. He felt that way about my family in general, although he'll say kinder words about my mother now. He says now that he felt my mother never put him down. But he didn't feel that way when she was alive, I don't think. From what I remember. But on Cindy's side is this man, with incredible, superior intelligence and knowledge and everything, and I, uhm . . . what can I say in a conversation with him without feeling like a total blob? Like a total piece of shit. Frightened. Well, he'd no more buy that than. . . . I've been telling him that for ten years. That my family's frightened of him. He thinks that's a crock of shit. Or, well, part of him thinks that. That's what he says. So I have to explain Jeff to her. Explain Cindy to him.

Perhaps I should just get out of it? Shut my mouth? What would happen? I think maybe . . . well, it's my bag. It's my own thing of wanting everybody that I know to dig each other. You know, if I dig him, and I dig her, or somebody else, my family or friends, and they don't dig each other, then I'm forced to choose. The way I did with Jan, in New York, which turned out so awful. Jan was this really good friend I had in New York, that Jeffy couldn't let me be a friend to anymore. Now, other people apparently can go along. If there's two couples, and the men don't dig each other, or one man and one woman don't dig each other, the other people can still have some kind of relationship. That's not possible for me. I mean it was not possible for me with Jan. Because of Jeff. That had to end. Blatantly. He would have liked an end between my family and me, but he never pushed that. I could travel back to New York as often as I wanted when we lived in Boston.

That was true. Everybody was always very grateful to Jeffy. Terrific. Wonderful. You know, how many men would let their wives go back and stay a week with their family? Well, of course, that was superficially true. But underneath, he hated it. He hates it when I defend or make excuses for my family. Okay, my sister's a bitch, a hostile bitch. So she writes dumb letters. She plays mother to me. She does all that shit. Okay. In my life, I had two or three really terrific days with my sister. For me, that makes the rest worthwhile, because that's how it is in life. You get a couple of moments, and it makes the garbage worthwhile. And if those moments don't count, then forget it on the whole thing.

There has to be love or nothing good happens. No, that's not true. They don't have to love each other. I say, they have to understand. I feel anxious when it's Jeff and some-body else. See, you know how I feel about Jeff. Okay? Now I dig this somebody else, too. And there is tension between Jeff and Mr. Somebody. I don't know where that puts me except that it makes me anxious. It's very difficult for me. I feel the difficulty. Whether he's putting it on me or not, I can't say. I can't say that with any objectivity or justice. I don't know whether it's him or me. Other people have said it's him. That was the hang-up which split my friendship with Jan. Connie has been very cautious, and she has hinted at the same thing. Other friends also hinted about this thing, too.

And then I'm caught in the whirligig of agreeing with them. But not wanting to out loud, because that's betrayal of Jeff. You understand? You must, or you would have hinted that you feel it, too. Except you wouldn't have hinted. You'd have thrown it right at me. Since you haven't, since you know Jeff is jealous of you, since you know it isn't the money but the excuse Jeff uses because he's jealous of you, I figure you know. You understand.

157

See, with Myrna it was different. Myrna didn't crap around. Myrna and Jeff had their own relationship. The three of us had our own thing. She and I had our own thing. And all of them could merge. It was okay. It was straight. Myrna could let Jeff have it straight. She would say to him, you've got power, and you know it; when you walk into a room, you've got power. And Jeff would accept it from her. The same kind of power you were talking about, doc, when you told Grace she had power, when Maxine overreacted to something that Grace said. And you said to Grace, you see that power. Well, you know Jeff's got that! Nobody else could say that to Jeff. But Myrna said it.

Straight out. Flat. He didn't like it, but he knew it was true. Or he did like it. It was one of those, uhm . . . ambivalent things. Myrna was a very real person. Myrna was. She died while we were in New York. We had returned from Massachusetts to live in New York before she died. I guess she's been dead about two years. She was about forty when she died. Or just turned forty. I don't remember.

Myrna was an illegitimate child, like Jeff. And her mother didn't want to marry her father. She didn't want to. But Myrna grew up in a very warm family atmosphere. She never knew her father. There were some little bits of information she got about him. There was some indication that he might have been part Cherokee, which she kind of liked. And she did kind of have an Indian sort of nose. She grew up reared a Catholic. Was it Stillwater? Some little Minnesota town, something like that. With a lot of uncles and aunts, too. Her family was very close, and very warm, unlike Jeff's illegitimacy. Jeff had a rotten, cold childhood, being emotionally abandoned by Muriel and physically abandoned by his true mother.

There was a bond between them, Jeff and Myrna. I told you once she gave him a birthday present. Listen to what she wrote on the card. It said:

158

Dear Jeff,

Never mind that it could have been more efficiently done, I'm glad you're here.

Love,

Myrna

It was really nice. His childhood was shit, and hers was warm. They really had a bond. I don't know what all made it a bond. Jeff would have to tell you that. Their bond didn't get between Myrna and me, though. I met Myrna through Jan. I had met her briefly at some party with the New York crowd, on one of our visits back from Boston. Anyway, one Christmas we had come back. It was before Gilbert was born. Before I was pregnant. And . . . uhm . . . maybe I was pregnant. I'm not sure. And we . . . how we used to do when we came back to New York was . . . I used to maybe come out a week ahead of time. Stay with my family. Then Jeff would come up, and we'd stay with Jan and Robert. Robert was Jan's husband. He was a poison mixer by profession. I just remember this one day. I guess it was after New Year's Eve. Uhm . . . New Year's Day. And I guess we were gonna leave the next day. A whole bunch of people were up at Jan's. Myrna was there. Myrna was in Jungian analysis. She had been for years. She was married when she was like nineteen. They were married for something like seven years. And when she split, she went to Zürich, to whatever that place is in Zürich.

She did the Jungian bit there at their main analytic institute and came back and continued with the whole . . . you know, that cult. That whole business they get into. Anyway, we rapped. This was really the first time we met. I used to write huge tome-type letters to Jan. You know, four or five typewritten pages. They were like journals. She would do the same. And Jan had shared some of these letters with Myrna. And Myrna said to me, I hope you don't mind. And I said, no, of course not. And she said, when I read those letters, I wanted to know you so much. If I wrote to you, would you write to me? And I said, sure.

So we began to write after we left for Massachusetts. That was in January. In March she . . . she was always in the business, writing for magazines and newspapers and those places . . . and she had a vacation and she wanted to come out for a visit. And we thought, yea, great. This was before Gil. It was before I was pregnant, too. I'm sure now. And so she came out. She was very frightened to come out. I don't remember the letters we wrote, but at that time we still didn't really know each other. She was very frightened. She wasn't asked to come out. It was super. It was so fantastic. It was just so great. And she stayed for a week. It's . . . I . . . uhm . . . it's hard to talk about her. I still can't not cry about Myrna. It gets wet in here, as I've explained.

We took her to the airport to go back. Myrna was a big gal. Maybe five-ten. Very earthy. And she had kind of blond hair and this . . . uhm . . . this kind of Indian nose, and . . . uhm . . . kind of a rough skin. Pox marked. She was always going to people for her skin. Oh, she was just real. And she had very slender arms with very slender hands. Curious. The rest of her was very earthy. They weren't ethereal or beautiful hands, in any way. They were kind of long, slender . . . weird. When we took her to the airport, and as she was going through the gate, she came back and said, I can't go. It was really hard for her to go, and for us to say, look, you gotta go back to go to work. We'll see you soon. We are always coming back to New York.

While we were in Massachusetts. . . . That was the first visit. The next time she came down was so fantastic . . . she took off a year . . . it was a really hard time for her. She was somewhere into her interminable Jungian analysis, and she was trying to write a novel. She wrote tomes and tomes of journals. She was always writing down her dreams and stuff, in connection with this guy, Clovis Diamond, her

160

therapist. As she called it, working with him. You'd call it therapy and stuff. And so she had enough money to take off a year.

Her mother . . . she had hang-ups with her mother. Her mother lived in Rochester alone. They didn't live together anymore. She still had some hang-ups about her mother, who was a weird old duck. Just kind of a dumb-dumb. Her mother was just kind of a dumb lady. A nice enough lady, but you know, she didn't have a brain in her head.

Anyway, one time Jeff was away. I don't know where he was, Philadelphia or Pittsburgh or something; Gil was like a month old. And at midnight, our friend, Tom Hunter, knocked on our door. Now he'd been back to New York and had met some of our friends and fell in love with them all. It was a neat time of good friendships. So he knocked, and I said, who is it? And he said, it's Tom. I said, what do you want? And he said, uh, I got somebody with me and I though we'd come over and cheer you up, since Jeffy's away. I thought, oh, what the hell is this? So I open the door and it is dark. Just black. And I look at the dark with my myopia like Magoo. A figure steps out from the bushes by the door, and I say, hi, Lori. That's the girl Tom was going with. And the figure steps closer, and I yell, oh, my god, Myrna. She says, ya bitch. I come all this way for the weekend and you say, hi, Lori. And we hugged and kissed. She had made this deal with Tom for him to pick her up at the airport so they could surprise me. She came for the weekend. At that point, I don't think . . . yea . . . that was when she had returned to work and was making all kinds of neat money. So she had the bread and she felt, I wanna see these people. I wanna see Pammie. She never remarried and she thought, I got no responsibilities. So it costs some money to go there. So what.

And she came down for the weekend. Jeff came home the next day and found her there. It was wild. We got films. He took . . . he was on a film kick then. And we got these films of Myrna. I'm . . . you know, we're all slopped around, and I'm feeding the baby, and she's knitting this sweater for him, and we're all messy, and then there's booze glasses around. We're in our nightgowns. We're loving being together. And it's just really neat. Really neat.

And the third time Myrna came . . . uhm . . . then of course we saw her in between. Whenever we went to New York. And letters back and forth. I have all her letters. A lot of contact. And the third time she came, it was again for a weekend. She was on her way to Europe. She was working on . . . going to work for the director on some TV special about an island or whatever it was. And she came off the plane with all her clothes, and she had arranged that she was gonna work on the special, and then she had this extended ticket, and she was gonna stay in Europe for a year. She hadn't been back, I don't think, since that Zürich thing. And that had been some years before. About eleven years.

By the time we met her, she had been divorced maybe ten or eleven years. She stayed for the weekend. We also have films of that visit. Unlike before, when we didn't plan anything, when we just experienced each other, we had this neat party on this before-Europe visit. She had gone through this really rough time. And she'd been in a group with this guy, Clovis Diamond, who I think was also a Jungian analyst. They had this special kind of group. I think they called themselves The Magna Maters.

They were people involved in some artistic endeavor. Painting, sculpting, writing. Plus it was therapy and good friendship. Myrna knew a zillion people. The brilliance and the wisdom of Myrna, unlike myself, was that she never brought these people together. So before she arrived at our place in Boston, Jan had given her a going-away party. There were just . . . maybe a hundred people from the business; the industry; the Jungian crowd; Jan and her group; Judy, our witch friend; all of these people . . . incredibly different from one another. Always having heard about each other, never having met.

162

It was wild. And The Magna Maters and all of these people. And Myrna said, the love that had poured out to her from Clovis Diamond and his wife and all these other people, but especially from Clovis, she said,

God, I can see her so plainly, sitting across the table, crying. This beautiful person, wondering what she'd done to deserve it. To deserve the love from these people. From all of us.

Clovis Diamond, he gave the eulogy at her funeral. He couldn't do it. He just cracked up. He couldn't speak. He just stood up there and cried like the rest of us. I have to . . . uhm . . . I have a poem of hers. Judy and Roger, after she died, went through her poems. Some of us were gonna get together and make . . . you know, what do you call that . . . a private edition. But they didn't do that. That never happened.

So they just had one of her poems that she had written in those last six months done up and framed for her good friends. I'll bring it in. I'd like you to see it. If you read her letters . . . unbelievable. Well, anyway she left for Europe, for London. They were in England, shooting the TV special.

All through her life Myrna had affairs. And a number of abortions. She had this long affair with this married guy. This incredible love affair. Something . . . I don't know . . . something like when Irene talks in the *group* . . . sort of like Irene's love affair. I've forgotten Myrna's . . . I think his name was Nicholas. There was no question that he would ever leave his family, like in Irene's affair. Despite this, there was no bitterness there with Myrna. But she loved this guy, knowing he was married, knowing that. . . .

She was just so grateful for . . . she'd had this sick, rotten marriage. This zero marriage. Nicholas became her love . . . I don't know. Myrna was one of those people who, when she was nineteen, she was forty, and when she was forty, she was nineteen. She was something else. So she lost her voice in London. And those shit-asses down there told her it was the London climate. Fog. She got very weak all of a sudden. And she came home.

The surgeons opened her up. And closed her up again. And eventually it metastasized everywhere. Infiltration everywhere. The week. . . . We moved back to New York by then. The week before she died . . . she got most of her medication from Robert, who's a pharmacist. . . . But then Jan and Robert went on vacation, and Myrna was in intolerable pain. We knew. We knew from the beginning. Jeff and I knew. Not because she told us, but just because Jeff was in cancer research. And because our good friend Audrey Simon was an anesthesiologist. She and Myrna had met, and they had had their own moments together. And when we told her the little information that we got, Audrey reaffirmed what we already knew. Everybody else had all this hope and junk. And the chemotherapy . . . my god, Jeff was running the research shit in his own laboratory on the very medicine that she was getting.

Anyway, Myrna called me. She was living then with Judy and Roger those months. Judy called, or Roger, or one of them called and said I had to get this medication for her. Her doctor was across from Sinai Hospital. So Gil and I went. We got the stuff and drove it down to them. And I saw her just for a few minutes. She was very tired and in terrible pain, although she never let on. And I remember I went out and got some food for the rest of us, and she retired to bed. A few days later, Judy and Roger called and said she'd gone into the hospital. And Myrna had been going through the yoga stuff with Judy. And the exercises and all of it. That was Judy's way, I think, of sharing Myrna's struggles and hopes and acceptance of the coming end. The physicians said they were gonna keep her for a week and send her home. You know, according to their rules about the way this stuff goes, there was no reason—no reason, ha, it's really ironic—no immediate reason for her to die then.

But it was Judy's feeling that Myrna had decided to go then. And so she did. See, there was a hassle about where Jan and Robert were. Myrna and Jan were extremely close, and Robert, too. And they were away up in the woods. Gone to Ontario, and nobody knew where they were. We had the Royal Mounted Police out looking for them and all of that. And then there was the thing . . . Judy wanted just to have her cremated, and have a simple service at the Yoga Church. But then Myrna's mother wanted the Catholic thing. It wasn't really a Catholic . . . I don't know.

She was buried at a Catholic place, but her mother wanted a regular open casket shit. Judy just couldn't fight it with the old lady. So, she said, okay. Then finally, however it happened, I've forgotten now, Jan was contacted. And Jan called me from wherever they were on the road. The funeral was to be the next day. The funeral was horrible. I just . . . I told Jan, I said, look, and I told her the circumstances of Myrna's death and what Judy had said about Myrna choosing to go.

It was awful . . . it was just awful. I remember I couldn't stop shaking and crying. That's all I remember . . . how awful. And the crying. Anyway, I told Jan it was imposs . . . I told her she wouldn't make it for the funeral, and besides, the funeral was not where it was at anyway. Whatever I said, I made her feel it was okay not to have to try to get to the funeral. I promised her I would take her to the cemetery when she came back.

And so Jeff and I went. And, indeed, they had an open casket, though most . . . none of us looked in it. We all sat in the back. And Clovis Diamond cried. Then we all drove out. Way out. And they buried her on top of this grassy place somewhere. And when Jan got back, I took her to the cemetery. And it was a month or so after that when Jeff and I split our friendship with Jan and Robert. It was too much to explain Jeff to them. As well as the other way around. . . .

SIXTEEN

A WEIGHT IS LIFTED

I HAVE A PRESENT FOR YOU—ME. Yep. It's me.
Would you believe that I have felt really terrific for like
three days. Just really wild. Neat. Beautiful. I'm flying
higher than a kite. It's so perfect. Get out your little note
pad and write it all down. Uhm . . . now listen, I'm going
to say something first. And then if I digress, which I'm
liable to do, 'cause my mind's going like bombs, you get me
back to it, 'cause it's something I want to think about.

But it all started . . . it's really weird . . . when I left
here Tuesday from the *group*. I thought about Grace saying
that I frightened her. And when I got around to reacting
to that, which wasn't really long, considering how long it
usually takes me, I started to giggle. And I just felt terrific.
Just really funny.

I was giggling all day. I even called Jeff, which is something I rarely do. He usually calls me during the day. But
I called him, and I said, I feel really good, and I thought I
better share it with you, lest it dissipate by the time you
come home, which it didn't, fortunately. I just thought I'd
share it with him during the day. He thought I was nutty.
Delightfully so. And he was very pleased that I had done
that. And so was I.

God, Tuesday night I couldn't even sleep. My mind was
going . . . exploding in a zillion different directions. It was
wild. Just really wild. And it had to do with what Grace
said. Grace said I frightened her, right? Remember that?
I think I tried to explain some intimate stuff Jeff and I
had done the night before, and I think she said it after

I said that. Am I right? I don't quite remember. Maybe she said it before. Or after. What I think is that it was the first time that I have felt real feedback from somebody. Not just in the *group,* but everywhere. Now maybe I've gotten it before and not heard it. I don't know about that.

But this is the first time that somebody didn't say, oh, you're terrific, or you're wonderful, or you're a piece of shit. Or any of that junk. None of that is very meaningful to me. But Grace used it like a real word. A real response. A specific, description kind of thing. And I don't really know, in all of my thinking about all of this whether . . . what the word frightened means. Whether it has to do with me. Or her and me together. Or her by herself. I don't really know that, and I don't really care. I do care, but that's not too important to me. It was just really neat. It was, uhm . . . it was some real thing. Like power. Do you get what I mean? Well, I thought about . . . I thought . . . I started to giggle when I was driving home. I thought, yea, I've got this power. To frighten, one must have power. But I don't think that's what really turned me on.

I think it was simply the fact that somebody had a response. That there was a specific . . . this kind of word. I remember you asked her right then if she could say it another way. I think I even tried. Maybe my intensity overwhelmed me. But she stuck to frightened. I don't know what to make of that. I'm not sure what to make of my response to it either, except I'm enjoying it a lot. And the fact that it has lasted this long is just incredible to me. With that . . . uhm . . . maybe part of it is that my reaction to some of these things in the past was not as prolonged as now. This is what I've come up with. . . . Wait. Let me back up.

For a long time, I haven't felt what was happening, what was coming out of all this therapy, and the *group,* and the whole thing. I just felt like nothing was going on, like it was just a big limbo. And then I think this, and a lot of other things. I suppose I suddenly realize how long it does take me to respond. Now I can sit and rap; just boom, boom, boom—like that. But that's all it is. It's not really saying anything. It's just, uhm . . . oh, what did Jeff say when I was talking, something like I talk with no substance. That I talk gossip, garbage.

I've mentioned it before. Just how long it takes me to respond. Say, in the *group* thing. If somebody says shit, you know, it might take me till later Tuesday night to suddenly find my feeling about what she said. And how I feel about responding to it takes even longer. Well, this delay didn't happen over this thing with Grace, Tuesday. It was different. And I was not . . . I have not been aware of this, ever. That's how I've been. That's how I've been operating. And I'm still doing it. But at least I've come out now to where I can recognize and say to me, oh, look, here's what you're doing, right? Grace said something else that day, also. But to that I had a long lag response, compared to her saying she was frightened of me. It was when I said something about Linda just dropping all this really deep, terrible stuff, like toast and tea. Like it was . . . what, zilch. And Grace said, sometimes you have to tell about those awful things like toast and tea, because there's no other way to talk about it. Or it will just tear your guts out. And I remember nodding and thinking, yea, right, I understand that.

But then, later . . . I agree with that intellectually and know we all have to do that for survival, but uhm . . . not in a *group* therapy, not in a private session, not in an encounter group, not where you're coming specifically to let it hang out and to feel it. And to learn to know what you feel. And once you know what you feel, then go ahead and reverse it. Then feel what you know.

If it happens on the outside, in one's daily life, when those kinds of incidents are brought up when you're having coffee with somebody, sure you talk about it like toast and tea, because there isn't any other way to talk about it. It's too horrendous. But not in here. Least of all in here.

I happen to be of the feeling, least of all anywhere. But I can understand that we all do it, as a giant defense. It might even be good to a certain extent. But see, I couldn't say that right away. I had to work it out because I'm . . . uhm . . . it's so funny that Grace used—see, these things are tied together—that she used the words frightened of me, because I am intimidated by Grace. I'm frightened of her! And so I think it's the intimidation, in addition to my long pattern of just not spontaneously responding.

We should come here for saying, no, damn it! Here's where Linda ought to say, oh, God, my old man tried to make a pass at me. I'm thirty-four years old, and he comes at me in the living room, and he's nude! I'm shivering, and she's talking tea. The way she went on, so casual like. Making excuses. What was it how she put it, my father was probably asleep, he didn't know what he was doing when he reached up my skirt, he probably thought I was my mother. Then to say, like she could care less, while she sits there, former Catholic that she is, six months pregnant, married to her husband, the rabbi—God, it's not real! Her big belly as proof, and she whispers like, so what, my father threw me out of the house after this happened. He had to because he told my mother I undressed him when he was sleeping. I was about to puke when she really defended him with all her understanding. Her father's trying to screw her. Then he throws her out of the house, and she says, I can understand why he's like that. My mother's frigid, and he never gets any from her.

Well, doc, like they say, whoever the hell "they" are anyway, it's better to give than to receive. So Linda gives. And she says it with no expression or feeling. That's not so. She had a smile. And it happened last summer! Her kid could have walked into that scene, or her husband even. Well, shit, to hear her, it's like tea. She should feel something about it. I mean whatever . . . I don't know. I've told you before, when Cindy said that about my father, you asked me, what did she feel about it? Or maybe I

170

imagined you asked. Well, I haven't the faintest idea. She showed no feeling. And my friend Connie used to say it. Just lay it out. Flat. She used to trot out all the garbage in her life, to psychiatrist after psychiatrist, as I once told you. How her brother used to fuck her and make her suck him and all this stuff. Just trot it out, like toast and tea.

I didn't understand it then, and I still don't understand it. I think probably my way is to just block all that stuff and not to talk about it at all. But once it comes out, it comes out like a torrent. Maybe that's just me.

So all that stuff is going in my head. And then the other thing, I guess I didn't say it very well. . . . What I was trying to say . . . this heavy thought that Jeff laid on me, which I thought was really profound. I suppose what I mean is that, as an analogy, medical doctors in physical medicine go through this whole thing: medical training, and their residency, and everything else, and what they learn about is pathology, right? They don't learn about what it is that makes people well. Jeff once told me, a long time ago, that, in ancient China, people would pay their physicians to keep them well, and that if they got sick, the doctor had to really look out, 'cause he was in trouble. His job was to keep people well. Not treat them when they got sick. And I remember reading in the paper, when we were in Boston, that many of the doctors at some clinic in Texas were working on the early astronauts, the *original seven.* There was this fantastic opportunity . . . I haven't followed it, so I don't know what has come out of any of their projects . . . but to find out what is it that's health. That's what I mean talking about mental health.

Take Linda for instance. The various things that she has mentioned in her life . . . anybody . . . any schmuck could say, God, that's enough to put anybody in the looney bin. That's enough to make her sick. No wonder she's in therapy. But nobody can look at that life in between those awful incidents, or those incidents themselves, as she experienced them and did something about them; nobody

171

can say, that is why she's healthy and isn't at the looney bin. Do you dig that? Do you see what I'm saying?

Maybe I can do it better with another analogy. See, we talk about ghettos and environment. That's very big in our thinking for many years now. What it does to people. And God knows, it does things to people. Terrible things. But to get away from the generalization about that environment and how it affects most of the people in there, take an individual, Joe. With all of the horrible things that psychiatrists and sociologists and just everybody can say are pushing down on him in the environment, individual Joe makes it. I don't mean he goes out and gets a great job and all that, but that's part of it. He doesn't get pushed down by the horrible pathology around him. Somehow he makes choices in those tunnels. He makes the right choices to remain sane and healthy and a feeling human being. Constantly seeking to live, constantly seeking to feel. To be alive. Even though all this stuff . . . put it another way.

One can say, here's this and this and this in a person's background, and you can predict where a person's illness is gonna go. Granted that's very difficult. Far more difficult is to say, here's this, this, and this in so and so's background, and predict that individual Joe is gonna be okay. This person's going to seek help. This person's going to say, I'm not gonna be just a blob, I'm going to be real, even though Joe's whole environment was geared to determine unreality, on the part of the existence of this person. And that's what fascinates me. It doesn't fascinate me that all of the pathology exists and what it does to people—that doesn't fascinate me. It's the other that does.

And it was this kind of thing I think Jeff was talking about. He used other words, about determinism can go just so far in our understanding of a human being's life. We can't chart all these determining factors. But then, when you get to the bottom, there's human choice. See, in his particular life, he uses, about himself, the word pragmatic. It was always a word I absolutely hated. But

172

when he used it in this context, I could see what he meant. Jeff chose, here I am. He chose to say, here I am with my abilities, and with the limits on my abilities, from within and without. And he zoomed. Given those limits. Always recognizing those limits. Some of them very broad. All kinds of space. Some very little with no space at all. And seeing what he could do.

See, Jeff was born with a good physical body. His biological father had been what they'd called a natural athlete. How'd he know that . . . uhm, I dunno, but Jeff was the same. So he expanded on that in the weight lifting and track and swimming and the rest. Not necessarily in competition, but really for his own self. And all other kinds of reasons like the physical defense against the hostile environment and shit like that. But he went to the ultimate with it, as far as the ultimate for him was concerned. Weight lifting is a really good metaphor for all of this, I think. We happened to catch on TV, I think it was on Sunday, or some sports program, the international weight lifting something or other. This Russian, they were the super heavyweights, this Russian . . . oh, God, they were unbelievable.

This huge man. The Russian. A lot of the guys were grotesque looking. He was not. He was well proportioned. A very young guy, in his twenties. Had a beard and stuff. This guy clean and jerked 501 pounds. Never, never having been done before, officially recorded. And he did it without the grunts and the groans and blowing that the . . . oh, if you could just see it! It was unbelievable! See, when Jeff was doing that, years ago, something like the highest was . . . I don't know, when Jeff did 320, it was breaking records. And now some ten years later, I guess it's more like twelve or fifteen years, this guy clean and jerked 501 pounds. And when you see that . . . I suppose for us. . . . I've only seen . . . one time we went to a weight lifting thing some years ago when we were living in Albany, and I remember one guy was from Maine. And as he was pushing the weights up, Jeff and I got so excited, we said, he's pushing himself

173

out of Maine. You know, it was terrific. It was what Jeffy did.

You know, he was Mr. Maine in 1950. Did I ever tell you that? It's true. Mr. Maine. Yea, I think it was 1950. Can you imagine? I think he was, what, seventeen. I was just a baby then. Those are long gone days. Can you imagine. . . . And see what I always dug about Jeffy, when I first met him . . . I used to have the fantasy about the Apollo figure . . . you know, the uh . . . everybody I knew was either all mental with flabby . . . just all fat. Or very physical and not much up in the head.

And Jeff combined these two elements in one thing. He went this whole physical route. Mr. Maine and the weight lifting, and after he got back from Korea, he ran the gym on the Navy base in Hawaii, and these kinds of sports and stuff. In Hawaii, he went the whole mystical route as well. He was in with a whole lot of mystical people. Old Hawaiian kind of mysticism. All kinds of occult stuff. Read every book he could get. All of this stuff. He went whole-hog into that. He was in one contest in Hawaii. I don't know if it was for Mr. Hawaii, or what.

He was up there doing the poses, and suddenly it dawned on him that this was ridiculous. He had been there. Many times he had been there. Why did he have to continue this? The occult just didn't give him enough answers. And he knew that physics, mathematics, biology; this was where he was gonna find answers. So he went into that. When he was transferred back to New Haven, he'd do his watch and then peddle on his bike across the ferry. He started taking courses at one of the state colleges, even before he was discharged. Of course the great moment of discharge was his coming across the ferry and taking his duffel bag of stuff, including the Purple Heart and all the rest of it, and dumping it in the bay. Gone—the whole schmeer. Dumping it in the bay, and that was the end. It was really beautiful. Must have really felt great. To end it with one big plop into the sea.

174

Well, I've had a zillion conversations in my head with you in the last two days, doc, and I had no idea I was gonna talk about Jeff and the whole weight lifting thing. I think . . . perhaps we are starting to make it together again. Yea. Probably, why, because last night I had an experience I have not had in a really long time. You know, you live with somebody and you love somebody. And the daily things and you go on and on. And every once in a while, far too rarely, it comes over me. And I suddenly feel love with such joy. Tremendous joy. Like it's a whole new thing. And I've experienced that with Jeffy before. But I haven't in a really long time. I guess I was coming on so strong, he thought I was crazy. It was beautiful. It was just really beautiful. I hadn't felt that kind of . . . overwhelming thing of, wow, I love you, Jeffy! Oh, it's really neat. Just great.

Another funny thing. You know I use the word neat a lot. I guess it was Tuesday afternoon, I went to pick Gil up at school, and one of the mothers brought in this basket of pug puppies. I thought they were so cute. I don't know her very well, but she used to drive Gil's bus. Her little girl's in Gil's room, and then she has an older boy, Virgil. I'm not sure how old he is. And Virgil has this deformed face. He keeps undergoing plastic surgery constantly. I don't know the story. I've never asked her what the underlying . . . half of his face is just really horrible, and he's such a neat kid. We sat and had cookies and stuff together at the Christmas open house. So Virgil dragged Gil in to see the puppies, and all these kids were around, and Virgil was there. And I said, hi, to them and then I said, oh, aren't they neat, when I saw the pugs.

And Virgil looked at me and said, I didn't know grown-ups used words like that. I was a little bit embarrassed, and his mother sort of laughed and said, she's not a grown-up. She's just grown big. And we laughed. It was so funny, 'cause Virgil was kind of serious. He was telling me about the dog and the mother. He said some phrase that was so cute, about the bitch and the sire. It was a really grown-up phrase. I wish I could remember it. And I said, well, Virgil, if I talk like a kid, you talk like a grown-up. And we had a big laugh over it. Really great. So neat. Neat.

I even was able, believe it or not, to put down the fear of the jinx. You know, the belief in the magic of words. Like, don't talk about it being good, or it will go away, right? And I've even been able to put that to rest a lot, so I was more able to enjoy my love feelings for Jeffy. Another thing. Wow, I'm moving. Another thing is that I'm learning, learning, just beginning to . . . to accept the evidence . . . how can I say it. . . . You know, I'm moving on a couple fronts. I tend to be very absolute, emotionally. When I'm not doing well, it's across the board. Everything is bad. Or everything is good. In all of this that has been taking place in the last couple days, I saw that I'm moving on all these fronts.

I'm becoming aware of my non-spontaneous responses. Looking at them. Seeing what they are all about. In the meantime, I'm still pigging it, so I'm not doing too well on the weight. But I decided, well, pick and choose. It's like learning about those space limits Jeff was talking about. Learning about who I am. Like that. Because, interestingly enough, I often. . . . I'm very much against the war. Never. I don't even listen to that stuff. And I don't look at it. I don't want to see it. 'Cause it's just. . . . But today this magazine came and it had a spread . . . this guy, Larry something, that great photographer, the guy who got killed. I looked at those pictures. This is stuff he took between 1965 and 1969. For the first time I looked at those pictures. Now I'm feeling good. High. I'm very high and I could feel those pictures. For the first time, I let myself. It was brief, but it was real. And what happened? I was able to go on being happy. On my own happy kick without necessarily feeling guilty. Maybe a little bit guilty.

Like learning to divide sort of, or learning to say, yea,

176

this is a part of me, and that is a part of me, and it's okay. I don't know how to say it well. Anyway, that just struck me as . . . listen, I couldn't . . . it's funny. . . . In terms of intellectually responding to my behavior about these photographs, or mentally responding to that . . . that took me an hour, until I got into the car and thought about it. That I was able to do that with the pictures. To look and see. But that's okay, because . . . well, it's okay that it took longer, because it was a real experience. In the experience, one doesn't have to analyze it.

And, uh . . . there for awhile, like last week I think it was, I was getting into bad things again with Gil. I was losing my grip. So he wasn't . . . everytime that happens, he starts kind of going to pieces. Not behaving properly and all. This week I just garnered myself again . . . this was even before *group* on Tuesday morning. I got myself going again with him. What I mean by that is being creative. Not just bouncing off. Being a creative person with him. Really, it's just amazing. All I have to do is just a little bit of it with that kid, and it's amazing. He just goes! Zoom, he's gone.

Jeff's old secretary in Boston sent him his old abacus. I don't know where she had it all this time. Jeff is fooling around with Gil, showing him the abacus. And then before he went to bed, Gil is doing all these neat things with the abacus. And, God, it was like watching Fourth of July. With this brain-booming, with these numbers. Especially numbers, as you know, is not my thing. And what Jeff said. He said, you see what Gil is doing, he is learning that he does it with the numbers. He said, I was in college before I realized that that was what it was all about with math. I remember, in college I had a glimmer of it in logic once. That this wasn't all just stuff that you got out of a book that had been written in stone a zillion years ago. These guys were creating these symbols on the board.

It was way beyond me. But it, the realization, was just wild. That Gil had this incredible power, flipping these

177

little things, making sets and junk. It was really neat. And then, you know, we had another nice thing happen. Different from what usually happens. Everytime he spills something, I go into a big scene, why'd ya spill that, bla, bla? Well, he was having lunch at the dining room table, and he had a glass of water. And I went to do something and I dumped the water all over. And I started to holler at myself, you ten-thumbed-jerk. And he started giggling and laughing.

And I said, it's really neat to see a grown-up goof, isn't it? And do the same things I holler at you about? And he said, yea, it's great! That was a nice moment. So funny. . . . I'm exhausted. What a session.

What else did I think about that *group* thing? There was something else, uhm . . . back to the . . . I don't know about the frightened thing. I don't know why that set me off, really. I've said some things today, but I don't really know. I was just . . . I can just remember . . . it's something I'll probably never forget. It's one of those kind of moments that just stick in your mind. Even though Grace touched something important in me, it was total. See, I got a lot of funny feelings about Grace. I don't know if I should talk about it in here, or if I should get up the guts to talk about it in the *group* with her. A lot of funny things with Grace. Weird.

It was often, not recently, but in the beginning weeks, when I joined the *group*. . . . You know, the *group* had been in progress and I was an interloper then. She reminded me very much of Myrna, like when I became part of a crowd that already was. These two women had the same kind of reality. Grace struck me as so real. Lately, I've kind of lost that feeling about her. I feel like she hasn't said much about herself in a really long time. But it's sort of hard in *there*. There are a lot of us, so it's hard for everybody to get a turn at bat, to use your phrase. And I'm mixed up about my newer feelings about Grace.

As long as I've mentioned Myrna—was it last week that I did that whole number on Myrna? Was it? See, I felt strange when I left here. I was shook. I went to the hall bathroom after leaving your office and had to stay there for awhile. Then I thought, I don't know . . . I guess what I thought was, I don't know how much you learned about me from what I told you about Myrna. While I told you a lot about her, what, if anything, did I reveal about me? So I felt funny about it, because I tried so hard, for a change, to stick to the chronology. There was one thing that I . . . well, there were a zillion things that I didn't mention. One especially that I thought about afterwards. It seems that I told you this before.

One time, I'm not sure quite when this was. Whether we were in New York living or if it was on a visit from Boston; I think it was a visit. Yea. It had to be. Myrna came over. I was staying at my folks. Mother got to talking about communism or some garbage and I was trying to just give some information. As they used to call it in Synanon, run some information to my folks, about things. And Myrna used to really get hot-under-the-collar at anybody who was at the opposite end of where she stood on any question. And then we left the house. She and I went out to eat. She said, you were so incredible with your parents. I said, what do you mean? She said, you were so patient with them. See, my folks were really saying garbage things. I said, well, yea. And she said, oh, my God, don't you know who you are?

Well, that's a present that people rarely give a person. And one of the . . . the other special, special thing that Myrna gave me was when I returned from New York after the visit that we made when Gil was six months old. Things were really horrible at that time between Jeff and me, and I didn't know which end was up. And I called her at nine o'clock in the morning, Boston time, so it was seven in New York, I think. Some special defense time shift that was temporarily in effect. I told her, I didn't know if I loved him anymore, and that I didn't know what was happening. Jeff and I had gone into what has now become

179

one of our periodic wing-dings, but which was new then.

And I had been carrying around these two shrinks' names, which Olson had given me, before we left New York for Massachusetts. For three years! I never called them. I just carried them in my wallet. And Myrna said, look, you got those names from Olson. You call yourself a psychiatrist now, before you're too crazy to know whether he's any good or not. And that struck me so great and so real and so funny that I did it. I just hung up and I called Rosenberg. Immediately. I guess a day later I told Jeff that I had done it, after I went to see Rosenberg. It was sort of funny. I mean, God, what a marvelous thing to say. One of the all time beautiful things to say, *before you're too crazy to know if he's any good or not.* I thought it was just terrific. Nothing else could have gotten me to do it.

Holy-hell, another note for Jeff. What is this? Arabic or modern art? Since you write so bad, can I read it to see if he'll be able to read it? Because you're not legible at times. Okay if I read it? Huh? Is it?

Dear Jeff,

In five weeks, I will have an opening in a group for married couples. I feel that I need the couples' group to do my best for you as a husband-wife team. While I do not feel it is always wise, Pam always defers to your wishes on joint issues. She indicated the decision for group therapy is yours alone.

The future rests, as I see it, upon you—as much as upon Pam and me. Since you call the shots, this note is for you. Perhaps Pam can carry a firm reply, yea or nay, to her next Thursday session.

Dr. Becky

I don't know what to say. It's a nice . . . it's really interesting, 'cause yesterday we went to our Spanish class, and

I just sort of briefly . . . I started to discuss with Jeffy a little bit about what I was discovering about myself. He'll love your note. This lag or gap in my response to what happens. We were driving to Spanish, and he said, you're really getting somewhere with yourself. Something to that effect. He said, I envy you. And I said, now, God, I must be high, or I wouldn't have had the guts to say something like this three days ago. I said, you know, it would really be nice, when I get around to dropping the private sessions, if the two of us could be in a couples' thing together. I think it would really be neat, using my favorite word. And you know what he said? He said, yea. Isn't that wild?

You never told me you did E.S.P., doc. But you know he's gonna talk to me about money. If Jeff says yes, I would want to tell the women in the *group* that I'll be leaving in a month to enter a couples' group with Jeff. Is that okay? I mean I really would feel funny busting away from the ladies' abruptly. You do want me to stop in the ladies' group, don't you? Oh, I'll miss that. But . . . so I'd have my private session, and Jeff and I would have the couples' group together, and I'd drop the ladies' group. Oh, wow. And he's in a . . . I better wait. Well, today I feel really good. Up until this week, I thought, hey, lady, you're not really working in therapy. I used to be a hard worker in therapy with the other shrinks. And I felt that I'm not doing it. Now I feel like I'm doing it. I guess I'm just impatient. But somewhere along the line, I find out, like today, that I have been working. That I have been doing it, and it's really neat.

Wow, that hits hard. I'm already feeling responses about leaving the ladies' group. But I've got a month to work that through. It's all sort of scarey. Maybe he'll dig it. Who knows?

SEVENTEEN

A CRY TO CONQUER

JEFF SAID IT'S *NO* FOR THE COUPLES' GROUP! So I have to regroup myself. Reorganize myself. Or something like that. I said a lot of ugly things to him about it . . . I don't want to talk about it. Crap. I said to myself, look here, you've got to start digging in, Jeff is out, no help there, so you better find out what you're doing here.

And I've come up with this. I'm not concerned about the private sessions. I'm mostly concerned about the *group* because that's a whole different thing. That's where I think a lot of the new stuff for me happens. You know that, despite all my therapy, I've never been in a *group* thing before. And in contrast to Margaret, who thinks of herself as sick, I don't think of myself as sick. And I'm not here to get cured, or to get well, or any of that shit. I just want to find out about feelings.

I should back up a little bit. When we left Tuesday, many of us felt rather strange. I don't know if I'm . . . uhm . . . well, in any case, in the lobby downstairs, Margaret stopped me. Actually she started talking to me in the elevator. I felt a little uncomfortable about it, because I know your rule about not socializing outside of the *group* and not rapping outside and stuff, though most of us rap, but we don't usually say too much. She asked me if I was really serious about what I said about you. You know, the bit when I said that just because you got a gillion diplomas and stuff on your wall doesn't make you perfect or always right or whatever. That you're . . . a person. Something like that.

So I told her, yea, he's a real pro. He's very good. There are people with less degrees that are maybe better. People with more degrees who are worse. And she kept on, into the lobby. See, I don't remember all Margaret said, but a couple of things were sort of strange. Like when she said she was not sure what kind of neurosis she had. And whether she was getting well. I suggested maybe she should use a different language. Who knows what sick is anyway—or well, or neurotic? And Margaret said, I want a vacation from therapy, but it's sort of presumptuous of me to suggest it. What she meant was presumptuous in terms of you, the doctor, being the one to suggest it, because she thinks you know all, do all, and all that shit. I really had to laugh, and I said, no shrink in the world is gonna tell you you need a vacation from therapy, whatever the hell that means. Her thinking you're God, though, really is a laugh.

I just kind of told her how I viewed things. And I've used this metaphor before, because it's meaningful to me of . . . uh. I asked her if she'd ever jumped from a high dive. And she looked at me frightened and she said, no. She said, I jumped from the edge once. And I said, it was scarey, right? And she said, yea. I said, did you do it? And she said, yea, I did it. And I said, well, we can also say a whole lot about what it's like to be in the water, after having jumped. But it is my belief that one can't say much at all, if anything, about what happens in between. But that once you're in the water, you have done it. I guess Victor Frankl talks about that . . . it just occurred to me. . . . Anyway, I told her, you can look back and talk about it then. But you can't talk about it any other time. You can look back and say, I did it. I don't know if that was meaningful to her.

Like I said, I was guilty for breaking your rule, so I went off and said good-bye and went into the pharmacy. My feeling was . . . Helen had said to me as we walked out, do you feel strange about the session? And I said, yea. And I suppose that I felt much like what Helen felt.

184

That I, too, want some contact with these people. Little had been made in the *group* session. I thought later that I should ask for a refund. Then I thought, well, if I want contact, then I should do some contacting. So I kind of settled for a rain check. Even as it was going on, I thought I'd better work hard to get something out of that session. The main part that I got out of it was watching Grace with those incredible defenses. I could see how I must look when Jeff and I engage in certain rotten conversations. When my defenses come out, boom-boom-boom, like that. And how awful it is. How really awful. Uckk.

I think Helen's word was right—disgusting. And then I thought, why? Why didn't I care about what Grace might have been feeling? Obviously, she is troubled. Obviously, she had terrible pain. She came on different for her, sort of in the same way Margaret comes on all the time. And I've sat in there, as many of us have, for weeks—banging at Margaret's wall. But I had no interest in banging down Grace's wall, really. Maybe it had to do with what one expects of people after knowing them a little while. One expects the wall from Margaret and one can feel that, behind that wall, there is somebody there, so it's worthwhile to chip away at it. Not all the time, 'cause it's a bore. Not all the time. But some of the time it's not. Once in awhile you see a ray of light there. But Grace was always, to me, an extraordinarily real person. And then to see her being so secretive and defensive is just such a shock. A real disappointment.

Another thing that I felt; I hesitate to even bring this up, because it makes me feel pretty crummy. But . . . uh . . . I think it has to do with how I misread people. 'Cause I felt in there, maybe in our shouting match that, oooh, I don't want to go near that Grace. She doesn't like me. Plain and simple. Not a very pleasant feeling. So it was really confusing. . . . There was the other expectation that it had been such a marvelous week for me with those three days of a high, one day of a real almost rock-bottom-low, when Jeff said, no, on the couples' group, but bouncing back and being rather pleased that I wasn't totally destroyed, as was usual for me. And in thinking again and again and again, about why Grace's comment two weeks ago, that I frightened her, had set me up so . . . and I thought . . . why it was that people respond, even if they say nice things to me, like you're terrific, you're wonderful, you're bla-bla-bla. In the reverse, I don't ever recall anyone saying what I did to them.

Using the language that way, saying, you make me feel terrific, or gee, you frighten me, or gee, whatever. Something about them, vis-a-vis me. And I really wanted to get back into that. Into those kinds of thoughts in the *group* last Tuesday. And when Grace grabbed Tuesday and blew the session with her defensive shit, it was a letdown for me. Really weird. Frankly, I'm not interested in her divorce and crap. Everything she's ever said since I've been in the *group*—I don't know what she said about her husband before I got in—everything that she says now is all so hollow. And her other love. Crap. He sounds about as hollow as her husband. Maybe she knows that, too; maybe that's why she's defensive.

I'm beginning to feel really angry. Mad. Do I sound pissed? I'm not really sure it's Grace I'm mad at. Maybe Jeff. Maybe you. I said I experienced a low. It's true, I also anticipated it when you gave me the note. Everytime you give me a note for him, I anticipate it. And everytime, I say to myself, no, no, don't do that. Don't anticipate. Just go ahead. Everytime I go ahead, uhm. . . . I'm not gonna use my favorite phrase; we can just call it phrase number one. You know what I mean. Everytime, I get shit thrown in my face. I feel better saying it.

Jeff asked me this morning, it was interesting . . . I don't think I've ever heard him refer to you respectfully. He said, you don't need to tell the doctor my reasons for saying no. And I lied and told him, I already told him you said no. And Jeff asked if you asked why. And I said, no.

'Cause I told him I told you at the end of the *group* session and there wasn't time. I said to Jeff, or for Jeff, in terms of my wanting to let you know for your planning and for other patients, the answer is no . . . I just want to drop it now, okay? I could give you all his reasons, but you already know all his reasons. And all the reasons he doesn't say. And all the reasons I surmise are there, and he says that are there. Who cares? It's disgusting. The bastard.

Okay. I was scared to give him the note. And I waited for the proper time. What's a proper time? I gave it to him the evening of the day you gave it to me, I guess. I'm not sure. And he read it. And he turned around and went to sleep. There are more details, but essentially that's what happened. Nothing more was said . . . then. And so I started to zoom into a depression. The next evening was when we really talked about it.

He went and got the note. And his first response was, have you thought about this realistically? And I said, no, I figured why should I bother to think about it until I knew what you were gonna say. And he said, how can you pick up Gil at four o'clock and make it to the couples' group on time? Have you thought about that? I didn't want to argue the point. First I said, yea, I thought I could make it. Then I said, no, I probably couldn't make it. Then he said, have you thought about what you're gonna do with Gil? I said, well, I could discuss with Nancy, who does know I'm in therapy, for her to keep him for that hour. Or hire the kid who sits for us Wednesday nights when we go to Spanish. What would it cost? A buck and a half? He was pushing pretty hard. Okay, that was one thing.

The other thing was his time. Now it's true that Route 95 is torn up for most of its miles. Not forever, but now there are repairs on 95, and he talked *forever*. So it means he would have to leave work earlier, forever. Famous 95. In our home, a road becomes part of the family. A husband, a wife, kid, dog, and a goddamn highway. The cherry on top is what does he say to Mr. Bigboss about his leaving

187

early? Does he ask for it out of vacation time; the whole thing about the feeling of the people in the organization about people going to shrinks? Okay. Then there was another interesting reason. I mentioned I would be dropping the ladies' group and continuing privately. That was correct, right? And then, ha-ha, he said, I would feel. . . . He made sure I knew this was not a primary reason but nonetheless, it was a reason. He said, I would feel . . . Jeff said, I'm not about to go to couples' and then have you go into the private session and rake me over the coals. Because you're my shrink, right? As Jeff sees it, my shrink. Never to be his.

I think those were all the stated reasons. You know, so the level of the voices got a little high. I got a little angry, and I walked out. I tore up the note, and said I was pissed at you for giving me the note, and sticking me out there again. So that's that. And I don't want anymore notes from you to him. And I don't want to discuss with him his therapy. Or mutual therapy together, anymore. Or any goddamn therapy about Jeff. There is no way he's gonna do it. I don't think he feels that it would be beneficial—is my feeling of a reason unstated. I feel that he thinks it's a big bunch of sh . . . just a crock. Part of him feels that.

I feel sad, aside from feeling some increased task for me alone. You can't help Jeff if he won't come, but he wouldn't believe that in a million years. 'Cause you're my shrink. I've said some really rotten things about Jeff. So you can't tell me now that I continue, in the face of his fear of therapy, to look upon him as a God. The God. None of which he would ever believe. Besides which, I couldn't say it anyhow. One never talks to God that way. Given Jeff's no, I feel double, double responsibility to quit crapping around and get into the nitty-gritty here. And in the *group*. So, there it is. To steal from McArthur and T.R.—I shall return with a bigger stick, an even bigger stick.

EIGHTEEN

TAKING STOCK

I DON'T KNOW HOW I FEEL. I think I want . . . to continue from last week. . . . What I want . . . these feelings . . . it's a whole new language for me. This experience in therapy. It's not a language that I've ever used before in my life, or in my experience with therapy. And the *group* has done . . . uhm . . . I . . . several things. I want to be able to hear people. Really hear. Whether that means hear what they say, or hear what they don't say, or both. I want to feel the response. I want to close the gap of time in terms of what I feel, in response to what the ladies say or do or how they look. I'm tired of it happening twenty-four hours later, while I'm doing the dishes.

I want to know what I feel. I said this to Margaret last week in the lobby. I said, when somebody says something to me, I wanna know what I feel about that. Whether I express it or not to the person is another question. But I want to know what I feel. I. Me. And, see, often I don't. Or it takes so long to figure it out.

The other thing is that I want to be able to integrate what goes on in my head with what goes on in my gut, so it's a total thing. So that it's real. All this means real to me. That is the ideal I wish to approach in therapy and in the outside. And I'm gonna make it. Given that Jeff doesn't wish to participate in this sort of involvement with me, as we discussed about his not wanting the couples' group, I feel that if I can get on with this bit of work, that it will also help what happens between him and me. Even in the absence of his presence here. Now there are a lot of things . . . I don't want . . . let me start again. I'm not sure what I said two sessions ago. I was high two sessions back, right? I still feel in control of it now. But two weeks ago, I felt very strongly that I was beginning to pick and choose those things, so that I thought, terrific, I'm getting there. I just feel I'm coming together on that.

But there are other things in therapy that I'm still just shitting around on. Things that are very hard for me to do. Really hard. It's just a lot easier to shut off everything. The feelings and everything else. But, see, when I see people do that, when I see other people do it, when I see Linda drop her little bombs, when I see Grace drop her little bombs and continue to talk about crumpets and tea, I can't stand it. It makes me want to puke.

What is that? All right, it's people's defenses, and bla, bla, bla, bla. I don't have any tolerance of it. I don't have any patience of it. And if I'm doing it, I don't dig it for me either. Though it's as hard to see it in my own self, as it is for them to see in themselves. I'm an extraordinarily impatient person. I'm impatient with the dog, with Gil, with Jeff, with me, with Grace, with 95, with everybody. The *group* seems to be getting bigger and bigger to me. I find it really hard to *get* in there. But I will. So many silent people. It's hard enough for me to hear and get to know people when they are talking to me, and hear what they say, and pick out what's real and what's not real. But I certainly don't know what to make of their silence, when that's thrown at me.

I don't know what to make of it when they dump their stuff in their toast and tea—kind of style. I don't want any of that. I don't want to hear it. I do want to change it. And what angers me with my own self is that, as is usual for me, it's taken me two days to say that, when I should have said it in *there*, right then as it happened. I guess I was just plain scared. Because . . . see, when Margaret brought up that . . . that usual crap she drops, like I don't want to change the subject, but . . . and then she changes the subject. Well, shit, that's a usual thing that she does. Intellectual dung, that's all. And I thought, yea, let's talk about intellectual dung. I got sucked right in again, fool that I am. But you, doc, stopped her cold. Right in mid-sentence. And I realized, shit, I don't want to talk about any of this garbage either. This person and her wall and her kite and her bird of paradise and all of it. Blah. Then I thought, well, look, never has Margaret said one goddamn piece of real thing about herself. For months. Nothing. So why was I shocked? That was just a giant nothing in that Tuesday session. She stole Tuesday. That's all. It was really weird. She picked it up and walked away with Tuesday. Shoplifted Tuesday.

I don't like the moderation in dealing with feelings. I like the extremes. The highs, the lows. Any extreme becomes very real. I got to thinking maybe that's why I use the *in* language so much. Not to be dramatic, but simply to show or express how I feel in extremes. Certain words just do it better than other words. I happened to come up on the elevator with Helen the day of the last *group*. I knew she had quit her job. I knew things were happening there with Helen. You can just look at Helen and you know all kinds of real stuff is going on. Irene and Maxine don't even exist for me. I don't even know who the hell they are. Grace is a letdown . . . as she has been for some time now. Seems like a botched up deal. Indirectly, I suppose, it's fairly helpful.

Anyway, in terms of Jeff and me, it's important to speak of Jan. To return to her for a moment. I recall my concern was so big in me that I began to spill it out here in our very first session, and you had to call a halt lest I flip psychotic. And I never returned to her for over a hundred sessions—until recently. Probably then because of Myrna and not Jan. And it's taken all these many months to come back to that. Let me finish that thing with Jan. The break in our friendship and the events that led up to it built this huge, huge wall of distrust between us.

Enormous. It just feeds on old distrusts. Old images of, in terms of Jeff, images of, yea, right, a woman and a mother will kick you in the nuts everytime. Reject you everytime. Shit on you everytime. That's Jeff for you. And for me, there are my old guilts, of just being guilty. Live the guilt, feel guilty all the time. That's familiar, that's the way I operate. So that's what goes on. I keep going off the point about this Jan thing. . . .

I don't know how far back to go. I guess we met Jan and Robert, I think probably before we were married, through mutual friends. I was in envy of Jan for years. For all the years that I knew her. From the time when I knew her casually, to the time when we were very close friends. She's taller than I am. She's a dancer. Got this terrific body. A really sexy, attractive body. Except saggy boobs. Janice with the saggy boobs. That used to be the big joke among us, among our group of friends at the time. We got very close the last year or so, before we moved from New York to Massachusetts. Oh, God, I don't know if I can go into all this crap. Drag it all up. Uhm . . . Jan visited us many times in Massachusetts. And, of course, we stayed at their place many times when we came to New York. The big letters went back and forth. Jan was reading a lot of Zen stuff. She and Robert had split up several times. They had two kids. Jan was a nursery school teacher after . . . the time of the dancer had to pass . . . and oh, what can I tell you about Jan? She really had a body. The body keeps coming back.

Anyway, when we moved back to New York, the year in between Boston and coming here, Jan came down. Jeff found us a house, a neat house, and Jan came and helped me get the house all ready for the furniture to arrive. We had dinner at their place, and we had them over, and so on, and so on. You know, lots of contact. Jan had the tremendous ability to very subtly say things about Jeff, even about Gil, that were put-downs. Except, why I say "tremendous" is that I might be feeling Jeff got drunk at the party, and what a pain in the ass he was. Well, I might be feeling that, right? And she would say something in a real subtle way, like, you got two two-year-olds to take care of.

192

Kind of slow and underneath remarks. She had perfect timing. And it caught me, always, off guard. At times when I was pissed at Jeff. I never said, shut your face, don't talk about my husband that way. Because I had been feeling that . . . what she, uhm . . . would say. You know, it's the Cyrano thing again. If I want to feel that way about Jeff and have a rap with him about it, terrific, but you shut your face about it. But I never said that. Or she would say . . . Gil was especially difficult or demanding, and he was a hard infant to rear . . . he was alive, right? She gave birth to klutzes. This was Jan.

Physical, Jan, whose kids were born weighing two hundred pounds and didn't learn to sit-up till they were a year-and a-half; you know, couldn't walk. The whole thing. Yolts. I guess our problems started to surface when Gilly was six months old. I'm backing up now. Flashback. And things were really difficult with Jeff and me. Uhm . . . I was up at her house. I don't remember exactly when. I'd stay with my folks for a little while and then go up to Jan's. Jeff hadn't come up yet. And Gilly was six months old. He had just learned to pull hmiself up. This little kid used to sit in his walker and zoom around like the crab. He was sitting up, drinking juice out of his cup. Doing the whole thing. He was tremendous. He was . . . you know, alive. Doing neat things. But he cried a lot. And he spit up. And the whole bit that babies do. Well, Monica . . . she had Kristin who was five at the time, and Monica was born three weeks after Gil. Monica was what we used . . . what Jan called the no-neck monster. I mean she was just one huge blob, who could . . . uh . . . barely lie on her stomach, let alone sit up.

Well, the paradox was so incredible. Here I am, you know, old chunky Pammie who can barely make it across the floor without tripping. And a fantastic dancer, Jan. What has she got? She's got this blobby kid. And her older kid was also notoriously awkward as well. And I've got this kid, uhm . . . who's built like Mr. America and who's all over. It . . . it blew her mind. It blew Robert's mind. And part of it is that . . . Gil, especially then, not quite as much now. . . . He was the spitting image of Jeff. He looked exactly like Jeff. His body was exactly like Jeff's.

Well, who is Jeff? Jeff is, in that sense, extraordinarily, physically well-built. The whole physical thing that Jan was really into. But these little digs. . . . Well, then Jeffy came up to her house where I was. And things between Jeff and me were blowing up. Things were falling apart between us. It was awful, and on and on. We had fights . . . oh . . . it was . . . just ghastly. Anyway, Jan did an incredible thing! I drove with her to pick up Kristin from a birthday party. Jeff was still back at the house. She said, whatever she said, was to put me into the position of choosing between her, as my dear, close friend and Jeff as my husband. It was incredible! I told her, look, this is what you're doing, and you have no right to do that. Don't put me into this position. So that was kind of it. Right there. It was the beginning of. . . .

Jan had done this kind of thing with our other friends. Jeff and I weren't the only ones. It was her style to kind of knock people with an uncanny, silent, under-the-rug sort of punch. Like you knew you were bleeding, but it took awhile to find where she stabbed you. A velvet harpoon. Others felt it also. It gets so icky. Anyway, that was the beginning of the end. After that visit was when I returned to Massachusetts, to start with Rosenberg. I guess I sort of stopped writing to her. At least the tomes. I don't think I ever told Jeff how she used to cut him or make me choose or whatever. Not for a very long time. Not for many months, if I ever did. I never was quite sure if I ever told him what she had done. But then we were still friendly . . . unbelievable what a neurotic I . . . we were friendly when we moved back to New York. Well, what happened was, I guess we moved back, what in May or June? Whatever year it was, '68, I think. And I had a birthday party for Jeffy.

Myrna was still alive. She came with Roger and Judy,

but they didn't stay. Jan always had her little entourage of single men around. Her body was the draw. There was young Jimmy, who was an actor; Greg, her old boyfriend, whom she decided not to go with and marry Robert instead when she was nineteen, 'cause Robert had thirty-six thousand dollars. And I mean Jan and Robert were something. Their relationship was always the talk of everybody. So Jim came to the party, pretty Jim. And Jan's sister was in town at the time, having just gotten divorced. She came. Jan has two sisters and a fag brother, who is the queen of Greenwich Village, whom she will not recognize as being a fag. It's interesting. They both look exactly alike. Jan and her brother, the fag. Funny thing. I wonder whom the boys like better, Jan or her brother? They even sound alike. It was years later when I finally met him.

Anyway, the party went on. Jeff was very strange at the party. Partially because I kind of made it not only his party. I was bad. Oh, I did bad things at that whole party. I made it sort of . . . 'cause it was also Jan's birthday . . . a mixture party of birthdays. Jeff was getting a little drunk. More than a little . . . Myrna, Roger and Judy left. I don't know. I was caught up in the Jan thing again, doing the things like Jan. The grace. The style of her ways. What? She was, as I look back, a phoney woman's liber really.

Jan and Robert said they had another party to go to. Out in the valley. This guy's party who works for Robert. Robert's a pharmacist. I may have told you that before. A black party. I wanted to go. Black was not quite in then, and I wanted to go. Anyway, I left. I left Jeff on his birthday to stay home with Gil. I left to play games with Jan and Robert and Greg. Incredible! Oh, I could be so easily used by that woman; it was incredible. I did this rotten thing to Jeff. So we went. And we only stayed a little while and we came back. And Robert dropped me off. And I went in . . . through the back door. I went in to check Gil, and he wasn't in his bed. I went into our bedroom thinking, maybe he had awakened.

Gilly was only a little over two then, uh . . . to see if he had climbed in bed with Jeff. Nobody was there. Then I realized I walked past an empty driveway with no damn car there. And I panicked. Went in all directions at once. I didn't know what to do. Hey, I'm getting all wet here, doc. . . . Well, I called Jan and Robert and told them Jeff and Gil weren't here. And I knew Jeff was really drunk, and I was really frightened. I even called Judy and Roger. I thought maybe he'd driven out there. I didn't know where he could have gone. Robert said they would come right back over. And they came over, and I was panicked. I didn't give a shit about Jeff. I was scared about Gilly. That was all I could think about was my baby, back then.

Jan and Robert were there when Jeff comes waltzing in with Gil. And naturally Jeff was so furious to see Jan and Robert still there. He'd apparently . . . Gil woke up or whatever . . . so Jeff took him and wrapped him up and drove to the park. I think they even met some cop in the park who said friendly things like, what are ya doing here at this hour with a little kid? Stuff like that. And they rapped together. This cop and Jeff. Oh, well, that was it. That was really bad. Terribly scarey, and all the while Gil was safe. My guilt at the way I treated Jeff like shit was behind my fear and panic. That he did something bad to Gilly to get back at me.

And the next month, following that . . . Jeff and I went round and round again. I guess more than a month, because on Labor Day weekend, I took Gil down to my sister's. Jeff and I didn't go away. We stayed home. We stayed home to settle the moment of Jan and him and me. And we went 'round and 'round about Jan, until I got so drunk, I went in the bathroom and slit my wrist. One wrist. It's always just one wrist, doc. And I lay down on the floor, perfectly pleased to bleed to death. Oh, man, I'd never been so drunk in my life. I remember I had this dream or fantasy or what in the hell one has when they're that drunk. I was sucking Jeff, and I bit his testicles off. The penis stayed,

196

but the nuts came off. And I recall being surprised as hell because, while there was an ocean of blood, he didn't flinch. There I was, balls in hand, wondering what to do with them. Weird. The penis stayed. You know why a man's penis is referred to as a cock? Somewhere I heard that a rooster, or cock, led to the derivation. You know, how the rooster struts around? One boss-man rooster and his many hens. The cock of the walk, with red plumage . . . not plumage . . . that red stuff on its head, the blade. The toughest cock beats up all the other roosters, so he's the cock of the walk. Ruling rooster of the roost. It takes balls to rule the roost.

Anyway, I was so drunk. . . . I'd have to be really drunk to slit my wrist, otherwise it hurts too much, right? And Jeffy came in and found me there, and he cleaned me up. He really would have made a really good M.D. Later, one time, he said, that would have been the worst, to have committed suicide then, because it would have been about Jan. And I wasn't about to let that happen. So finally I had to make the choice. I had to say, fuck off, Jan! I don't know why it was so goddamn difficult for me. Everybody always thought that Jan and Myrna and me had latent Lesbian things anyway. Maybe we did. Anyway, I finally finished it. And that was the end. And it was a very difficult choice. And it didn't make a goddamn bit of difference, because Jeff has never ever forgiven me, and I knew he never would! He has never forgiven me and he still talks about Jan. To this day, if I want to see a play in Georgetown, or go to the theater, he says, ah, so you can write to Jan and say you've been doing all this stuff. God, it's been over two years since I told her to get lost! Two years? Can it be three? Three. Over three. Gilly's five . . . I guess it is. . . .

Choices. Goddamn lousy, rotten choices. So, doc, it's inventory time in the store. I've only a minute or so left today, so I. . . . Well, I've already said my goals—over and over. I want to feel. To be real. To examine me, in how I'm doing and being. Just to be rid of the crap that hangs on from the past and the now. That, of course, includes therapy helping my relationship with Jeff, which, like I said, I'll have to do alone now. If that's possible. I'm pretending it is, despite your note.

It's really just hitting me how scared Jeff must be of therapy. Not one . . . uhm, I'm not sure it had one thing to do with all the excuses he threw my way. What I think is that he can't admit that those many years he spent in therapy with Gladstun didn't really help him get his head together all that much. And he sees me getting my head together . . . so he's pissed at Gladstun or himself, and he doesn't know it. Maybe he does, down deep. He takes it out on you. Sometimes on me. He's scared to death of all . . . groups or crowds. God, he doesn't even like parties anymore. This all just occurred to me, and I feel stupid to have hoped he would come to the couples' thing. And you were even stupider, doc. Your optimism makes me sick.

But I love Jeffy. Good moments . . . a few really good moments have kept us going this long. And for me . . . well, I've been seeing you almost a year now. When I look up ahead, I panic 'cause I don't see any opening in the tunnel I'm in. But when I look back, I know it's helping. 'Cause I can't see the light from the side of the tunnel I entered either. So I'm in here, and I don't know how far in, or how far I have to go, and that's scarey.

I don't go around burning my hands with cigarettes. Which I'd been doing. I'm no longer a slave to the Jans of the world—as much anyway. I'm not as for always in the depression, with the bores, with the angries and the anxieties. I don't hate the *group* as much, or you for sticking me in with a bunch of heaven seekers, while I'm, oddly enough, the only one who believes in Santa Claus. Gilbert, he's doing okay. At times, beautiful. My guilts about him are less. I'm just feeling less like a big zero. Lots less.

Does that tell you anything, doc? Huh?

POSTSCRIPT

When you take this book into your thoughts, it is likely that certain passages have either awakened hibernating feelings or have aroused your interest in learning the outcome of Pam's psychotherapy, as well as a desire to know more "facts" about her life. For instance, where is Pam now? Has she achieved happiness? Was Jeff's decision not to join her in therapy a permanent one? How is their marriage? Is Pam, indeed, married at all? How is Gilly? Is Pam the terrible influence on Gilly she feels herself to be? Does this show up in Gilly as he grows older?

Unfortunately, these details of Pam's life are not available, as contact with her has been lost. She stopped therapy. Rather than deal with the frightening possibility that her marriage may not work out, or learn that it may not be all she wants to believe it is, she pulled away. Even her departure from therapy leaves certain questions unanswered: for instance, did Pam stop therapy also because of direct or subtle pressure from Jeff? Or was the decision solely hers?

The remaining alternative to achieving answers to lurking questions is to explain some of the psychodynamics—the psychological meanings—that are revealed by Pam about her character during the course of her therapy. With the background provided by the psychological explanations, fairly accurate educated guesses can be made about her.

There is no denying that Pam is a palpably alive and real human being, with so many attributes and so many foibles, that it is nearly impossible to escape recognizing some parts of your own life in aspects of her multifaceted character. You may identify with lonely Pam,

199

or loving Pam, or tender Pam, or raging Pam, or with any of the many other Pams. The huge array of significant people in her life may stimulate you to recall people in your life, similar to people Pam talks about.

There's Myrna. Poor Myrna, who had to die. And you think of a Myrna you know and that you love. Or Jan. Physical Jan, who may bring to mind angry feelings toward all the Jans in your world. And Hercules. What about Hercules, the huge, marvelous monster with the bad bathroom manners? The struggle Pam and Jeff have to find a noble name for this noble beast highlights the value friendship has for them. As soon as they learn their dog has the job of perpetuating old Herc's memory, the uneasy search for a fitting name is suddenly over. Hercules brings forth the romantic and the sentimental components of Pam, and it is one of the occasions when Jeff shows tenderness.

Maybe you see yourself in Jeff, who feels threatened that Pam may find another man to take his place with her. Possibly, like Jeff, you unknowingly control your own wife by making absolutely certain, just as Jeff makes absolutely certain, that she knows how hard you work, how much you dislike it, how difficult it is, or how smart you are to have the job you have. Unlike Jeff, maybe you are sufficiently insightful to know that, if you treat your wife this way, she, too, will feel guilty in spending money, because you let her know that you break your back to earn it.

Are you like the part of Jeff that is unable to express feelings directly—except for angry feelings? Jeff finds tenderness very difficult, if not impossible, to reveal, if Pam's portrayal of him is presumed accurate. Indirectly, by the naming of the dog, Jeff reveals great caring for Hercules' masters. Jeff's blood-shot eyes are a psychosomatic representation of his desire not to leave Pam for business travel. He shows tenderness, symbolically, by his eyes, but he cannot speak loving words. He also indicates soft feelings for Peru, an entire nation of people, but not for individual persons. The vast number of people involved assure Jeff that his expression of caring remains impersonal. Even Jeff's success with getting off Gilly's eye patch, an ostensible act of love, is done with all the finesse of performing delicate surgery with an ax.

The creative components in you may tune in on parts of Pam which are inventive. You may write or play an instrument or think original thoughts. You don't have to paint to feel like creative Pam, the painter. Do you wonder what her abstracts are really like? Do they have psychological meaning? Are her paintings capable of being interpreted, like dreams are analyzed? The answer is an unequivocal yes. Pam's pelvic paintings, the "uterus with octipi," and the "sperm painting," have very definite meanings. Through them, Pam puts her sexual dissatisfactions on invisible exhibit. Why the canvases contain sexual, as opposed to other emotional conflicts is highly speculative. The probable reason is that sexual problems are paramount. They begin around the later stages of Pam's pregnancy, and they mount to even greater heights after Gilly is born. Jeff feels relegated to second by an eight pound intruder, the first in a series of intruders, and Pam slowly becomes aware of Jeff's anger at both her and Gilly. The birth of Gilly is the starting point from which Pam recognizes Jeff's jealousy of anyone or anything that comes between them. The components of conception—sperm, egg, uterus—are splattered over many canvases. Pam's art work is her main mode of sublimation, a vehicle by which the tensions of sexual dissatisfaction with Jeff are converted into acceptable and rewarding channels. The paintings are symbolic products of Pam's unconscious, and the interpretation of abstract art is quite different from dream interpretation.

Certainly Pam's dreams are vivid, and, like all dreams, are packed with many meanings. The sexual connotations of the "Willy Dream" are obvious. Less obvious is Pam's wish to be young again, to be Cindy's age, and to start her life over again. The main theme of the "Bare Midriff Dream" is Pam's need to have a special feeling for Jeff, which she is unable to acquire. In waking life, she is angry with Jeff, and the idealized sentiments she desperately wishes to be able to feel for him are blocked. Pam praises Jeff to "Doc," and unrealistically expands his intellectual prowess to mathematics, to psychology, to science. She brags about powerful Jeff, the human dynamo, the natural athlete, the weight-lifter with the great physical strength of Mr. Maine. While protecting Jeff's image to "Doc" by making excuses for his demanding and controlling and irritating nature, she does two things. One, she builds up his image to her own self, and, two, she shifts the blame for *their* difficulties onto herself. Even with these "protective" mental processes, the idyllic feelings she wants to feel remain a sought-after goal. As a result, her frustrated feelings are dealt with in her sleep life, where she allows herself to dream, and to feel, in the dream, feelings which are not experienced when awake. Even during sleep, when her defenses are weakened, Pam's anger at Jeff prevails, and Doctor Becky becomes the recipient of the ideal feelings she wishes for Jeff.

Pam is Everyman, a conglomerate of human qualities which are simply and abundantly there. If you have a sexual problem, a weight problem, a marriage problem, or if you endure blinding frustrations, then you may step into Pam's shadow. When you do, it becomes nearly impossible to suppress the occasional feeling, "Hey, that's me. That's me talking. That's just how I feel." Truly, Pam has this quality, this Everyman.

What she does with her Everyman is the story of HALF-WAY THROUGH THE TUNNEL. She seeks and wonders, she searches and worries, she plods and plugs away, looking for that breakthrough. More than anything else, Pam wants her life to have meaning. She wants her interaction with others to be genuine. She wants to strip away the facade, the superficial grit. Only then will her life not be a waste.

At first glance, with all her robust language depicting anger and rage, with all her frustrations about herself and about Jeff, it is easy to believe that she seeks an *answer*—happiness. But she doesn't. She seeks *solutions* to problems that she feels, and the expectation is that the answers she comes up with will result in feeling a sense of meaning and worth and fulfillment.

To say that Pam *seeks* solutions is not completely accurate either. She is *driven* by a force which she cannot control. This force, this compulsive, propelling force overpowers her own will, in a sense, so that she *must* search for her own reality. This is not a selfish search where she accumulates and then discards used-up paper people. It is a gracious, warm interaction with others, and, at times, Pam has little conscious awareness about why she does what she does. Having seen five psychiatrists is a direct illustration of her need to learn who she is. Another illustration of this driving urge is found by examining her selection of friends. Pam gravitates toward people that possess traits and qualities she unconsciously feels she lacks. Jan is a tall, sexy, beautiful, graceful dancer, and, by contrast, Pam learns that she is neither tall, nor graceful. Yet, in a way, Pam comes to feel taller, since she is not cruel, not materialistic, and not an opportunist like Jan. Through Jan, Pam gains some knowledge about her own identity, and she also learns about foes in friend's clothes.

Through Margaret, Pam sees an image of the impervious, unreachable aspect of Jeff's personality. Pam learns, by pounding on Margaret's wall, that the hurt she feels is very similar to the hurt she feels when she pounds on the wall around Jeff. While Pam feels, "Oh, what a wall, what an awful wall," she derives from Margaret a better understanding of herself in her relatedness to Jeff. It is painful, but she learns how to take off a brick from the wall. Margaret is more than a transformation of Jeff. When Pam cries, "The whole world is a Margaret," her rage is directed at all people who erect walls to keep others away.

The *group* is another vehicle for learning, for recognizing, and, then, for understanding and solving problems. In general, group therapy focuses on interpersonal rather than intrapsychic interactions. By the carry-over of experiences beyond the *group* into the outside world, Pam learns from Margaret and the others how to deal with a vast array of problems. The group members seek help in overcoming difficulty in establishing and maintaining deep and rewarding relationships with others. Each member in Pam's *group* shares this common, basic problem, but it manifests itself differently in each person. Pam, like the others, tends to keep inside her hurts and disappointments. In this laboratory, this special microcosm of humanity, open, honest, direct expression of feelings is encouraged. The group members are voluntarily locked together for reasons of mutual help, caring and trust. Feelings of isolation within a *group,* or a fear of being misunderstood are common, but hopefully are short-lived. Pam feels isolated within her *group,* and she is very much afraid that if she is honest with the ladies about her marriage problems, they will tell her to leave Jeff. Consequently, she chooses not to be open with the group members about her feelings for Jeff. She decides to be dishonest, by bowing to her fear, and concealing from the *group* her angry feelings for Jeff. In her own thoughts, during her private sessions, she exalts Jeff. She places him above "their" husbands. She again makes him a superstar. She does not learn to put Jeff into her world, into a human world.

There is another meaningful component which Pam reveals in the context of the *group.* A process similar to sibling rivalry is present between Pam and the two new group members. She is vying for "Doc's" favor, and she unconsciously feels threatened that one of the new people will displace her. Pam feels that the two new "sweeties," as she calls them, receive protection that she does not, and she is angry. It is almost as if "Doc" becomes a father, who is to choose his favorite daughter, and Pam wants to be the one chosen. She wants to be regarded as special. She wants her attributes to be recognized. This particular group therapy process is in the haze beyond Pam's awareness, and she never learns why her feelings for the new members are distorted. Pam reacts to people outside of the group with similar, maladaptive feelings.

Pam is impelled to learn about herself, by comparison and by contrast, by loving and by being hurt, by involving herself deeply with many others. Her interaction with Myrna is a kind of closeness, a smashing together of ideation that is so potent as to border on the unreal. Pam learns here of her capacity for a consuming relationship. She learns what it feels like to have part of her own self die—when Myrna dies. With Scotty and Ivanoff, she observes reflections of her heterosexual self, while coming to terms with taboos born from her mother's don't-ever-let-a-boy-do-such-and-so warning. Pam's relationship with Cindy, beyond their daily contact, is a symbolic visit into her past. Through Cindy, Pam's sister, Sara, is brought into emotional proximity. The blood barrier is attacked again, as Pam tries to extricate herself from angry childhood feelings, and see Sara anew. From Cindy, and from Connie, and Linda, Pam is able to observe similar responses from three separate people who detach themselves from horrendous experiences by talking "toast and tea." Pam vacillates between understanding this, and continuing to wonder why they remain superficially indifferent. Being detached is so totally foreign to Pam that it is doubtful if she can really feel why people talk toast and tea. She can understand—intellectually—why they need to separate themselves from a traumatic event, but she can't understand this on a feeling level. Feelings quite opposite from detachment—involvement, intrusion, searching—characterize Pam. She cannot emotionally "go away" from the scene.

It is curious to reflect upon why Pam no longer feels her own guilt feelings for breaking the Seventh Commandment, when she expresses the tumultuous venom she feels for her mother and father. One reason that she blasts with impunity is that her fury at her family is diffused, and mixed into a complex network of hostility. Anger spills over everywhere: for Jeff, for the Margarets of the world, for beds that squeak, for allergy shots that don't work, for a world where she must pay to talk with someone. There is a second reason that the loathsome expressions directed at her parents no longer add to Pam's guilt. Pam has suffered sufficient hurt and pain from their *good intentions,* and her anger at her controlling mother and diddling father feels justified. Instead of guilt, there is hurt, loneliness, deep regret, and a sense of loss, for being unable to experience parental love feelings.

Not a small part of Pam's questioning her own authenticity has to do with her chaotic relationship with Jeff. After all, Jeff is her primary source of feedback, for pleasure as well as pain. When the input Pam receives is negative, she sees herself as a big nothing—a self-depreciating feeling of being a big zero. She despises the tense atmosphere with Jeff, with its garbled communication, and she questions why. She responds as if she is tied to an irritable, unpredictable, inconsistent, ever-changing bomb, which could explode at any time, and in any direction.

She feels the absence of necessary positives and the presence of unnecessary negatives in their relationship. Their togetherness lacks closeness, tolerance, understanding, and mutual respect. Much of the time, interaction between Pam and Jeff is dominated by mutual mistrust leading to an effort to control the other. A stressful, unpleasant competitiveness blackens attempts at relating warmly. The force of each needing to control the other is powerful, and cross allegations of sex "on your terms," or "who calls the shots" demonstrates this. They are rivals, not partners.

As HALFWAY THROUGH THE TUNNEL unfolds, Pam's defects are displayed, as well as her virtues. Contributions by Jeff to the joint problems between them are not as highlighted. One recurring lethal entity which Jeff unconsciously delivers to Pam deserves study. This maneuver is his saying one thing to her while meaning something else. Pam generally follows Jeff's explicit, spoken message, which is often different from his implicit, unspoken message. Being unable to reconcile these opposing demands, Pam feels bewildered. Obviously, she can't follow the explicit message without ignoring the implicit one. Either way, Pam is caught and feels caught in this *double bind* from Jeff. At times, Pam is aware of the *double bind*, but, too often, she isn't. When she is not consciously aware of being in the bind, she feels uneasy, confused and angry, even though she has no idea why she feels this way; only that she feels this way. As an example of a recurring *double bind* transaction, we cite the times where Jeff openly tells Pam that he feels she is doing well in psychotherapy, but the unstated, covert message that comes across is that her therapy is a waste of his money, and an inconvenience for him.

So, when Jeff conveys, "Go out in the rain and play, but don't get wet"—her stomach twists, she feels bewildered, uncertain, ultimately angry at Jeff, even without a cause that she can identify, and quite disgusted with her own self. "What am I to do? How do I come out of this in one piece? Whatever I choose, it's wrong."

The episode of *lovering* is another example of the *double bind*. If she allows Gilly to go to Jeff, Jeff gets angry. If she entertains Gill and keeps him away, Jeff gets angry. What is Pam to do to break the *double bind*? There are more *double binds;* for instance, when Jeff rejects Pam's acknowledging her confidence in him to make a living. He rejects Pam's optimism, and he also rejects her when she joins him in expressing concern. Jeff binds Pam, by blocking both alternatives.

This perplexing form of communication is very lethal to Pam, as it nourishes her neurosis. The *double bind* is equally deadly to Pam and Jeff, as a twosome, for there is no way that they can communicate meaningfully in the presence of muddled messages. Their lives are virtually infested with *double binds*—infiltrating and destroying mutual understanding and caring.

What can Pam do so that the cables don't cross? How can she learn if Jeff means *A* or *B* or both when he says *A-B*? Is there a magic formula to follow? How does she break a *double bind* once she recognizes it? Doctor Becky ultimately sends Jeff a note inviting him to enter therapy, in an attempt to repair the communication signals between Pam and Jeff, while problems between Pam and Pam continue to be solved. Without Jeff entering therapy, to help uncross the cables, and to solve the complicated communication equation, only a fraction of the problem can be solved, Pam's fraction.

Pam's growing insight into what is wrong between them, besides Jeff's reluctance to acknowledge his contribution to *their* problems, leads to greater and greater deterioration of their marriage. Pam's avowed unilateral effort cannot reap bilateral benefit, but only personal knowledge and growth for her. And the overflow from Pam to *them* is not sufficient to produce a mutually rewarding interaction. In fact, the more Pam grows, the greater the gap becomes because Jeff is standing still.

Jeff refuses therapy. He refuses to do just about anything to help their relationship, if it includes personal involvement for him. He is not to be inconvenienced. His commitment appears to be primarily to himself, his work, his image, his body, his knowledge, and his needs. He demands satisfaction of his needs by complaining, by being negative, and suspicious, and by *double binding* Pam at nearly every junction. What he does most often is bitch, and make it clear that he wants Pam to be a better fuck. About that, there is no *double bind;* the message is clear and direct. It is not out of premeditated cruelty that Jeff tramps on Pam, but nevertheless, he does. He uses her for his sexual needs; he uses her for his status when he speaks of his wife—the social worker, or when he declares to his peers that his wife—the artist—painted "this" to decorate a room at work. Jeff is unforgiving; he never forgets about the fifty cents Pam wouldn't give him for breakfast. Jeff excludes Pam; he rarely wants to go anywhere with her. Jeff is inconsiderate; he does not tell Pam *The Producers* is on television, when he knows she wants to see it. Pam is not without equal responsibility for their problems. She delivers a blow, some well below the belt, for every one she receives from Jeff. But, unlike her husband, she accepts her responsibility. She tries to better herself, and is willing to do everything required for improving their marriage.

In contrast to Pam, Jeff is perfectly lifeless—the antithesis of life-grabbing, life-gulping Pam. Pam tries so hard, and she comes up with—what—a wall. "Jeff's a wall," she says. And she experiences even more frustration in being unable to penetrate. The paradox is apparent. On one hand, as pointed out, Pam tends to deny the contribution from Jeff to their mutual problem. She takes full responsibility, for reasons already stated, and also because she knows, on some level, that when she depends on Jeff she meets with disappointment. On the other hand, Pam's denial of Jeff's contribution continually fails. Her position about either taking all the blame or sharing it remains in flux.

Pam, conceives new meanings to words—flip, *bouncing off, makes me crazy,* and she alters standard words—*sillies, friendlies, angries.* This is mainly a representation of frustration. She creates and accumulates new words for the reason that there are not present, in the English language, words which adequately describe how she feels. To talk on a feeling level, to make herself understood, to overcome the frustration of being unable to let out inner feelings, she hooks together new combinations of letters.

This same phenomenon explains Pam's overindulging, and excessive involving. Rarely does she do anything in moderation. She doesn't feel, she FEELS: she doesn't yell, she SHRIEKS. Even with her armamentarium of neologisms, she remains frustrated because she has many more feelings for which there are no words. Leftover feelings, which she has no way of revealing, are blurted out in obscene language. Angry feelings, rage feelings—feelings possessed by Pam that are so powerful that her search for expressive mechanisms leads her to profanity. Pam, herself, is not obscene, not vulgar, not profane. She authors a dictionary of the vulgar tongue to escape from the stranglehold of rage. Pam's obscenities are pure in the sense that they have cleansing, non-vulgar motives. They spell neurosis, frustration, rage; they spell war and killing, earthquake and death; they spell good-bye Myrna; good-bye to all the beautiful dead people in the world; they spell out that Pam can't make it with Jeff without professional help, despite enormous desire.

Part of Pam's problem, in not achieving the fulfillment she wishes, has to do with the gratification she receives from mere bits and pieces. Pam says, "You get a couple of moments, and it makes the garbage worthwhile. And if those moments don't count, then forget it on the whole thing." Unfortunately for Pam, she settles for too little—a few good moments. Because she derives such satisfaction from these samples of the good life, she never truly goes after greater fulfillment, sustained over a longer period of time. In a sense, Pam thrives on being forever on the edge, on being nearly counted out, on having the odds stacked heavily against her. Here is a view of Pam, living in deficiency rather than excess, here is Pam searching for a crack of light in the tunnel. Her "good" moments are just as excessive and expansive in euphoria as her deficient moments are shriveled in depression. She rarely, if at all, is the middle. She is forever the edge.

GLOSSARY

Pam uses certain words in a fashion peculiar and unique to her. These words require translation. Her vocabulary also includes many psychiatric terms which have become familiar to her during her many years as a patient. For those not deeply involved with psychiatry and psychotherapy, the following definitions may be helpful in understanding more fully the messages in HALFWAY THROUGH THE TUNNEL.

AMBIVALENCE—difficulty making a decision or knowing what to do or how to feel because of the co-existence of contradictory emotions.

ANGRY—feelings which are directed at a known object. See *hostile.*

BAG—an expression to indicate the presence of a problem that "belongs" to the person who has the problem, i.e., "that's his bag." In the context of this book, "bag" problems are neurotic conflicts.

BECKY—mispronouncing a person's name is usually indicative of angry feelings at that person, and is used in a put-down or derogatory sense. It is an indirect expression of anger.

BLOCKING—a psychological defense mechanism wherein one can't remember what he is just about to say; at times occurring in the middle of a sentence; at times between thoughts.

BOUNCING OFF—a word of Pam's creation, used when she recognizes that she attributes to others aspects of her own personality which she finds objectionable. In observing unwanted traits of her own self in others, she "bounces off," by seeing herself and not the other person. Unlike projection (see *project*), bouncing off is a conscious phenomenon.

BUG, to be BUGGED, or to BUG—to bother, to annoy, or to feel angry. As used here, the feeling of being bugged or the doing the bugging is a neurotic feeling or doing, as opposed to "just" being a pest.

CLITORAL ORGASM—a female sexual climax, felt by some to result from stimulation of the clitoris, as opposed to vaginal orgasm, or a total pelvic orgastic response.

CRAZY (as in it MAKES ME CRAZY)—feelings of frustration and confusion when someone or something real or beautiful is experienced; not knowing how to respond because of an unexpected "good." See *real*.

CYRANO SYNDROME—human interaction characterized by reversals; as when one asks for constructive criticism, receives it and then resents getting what one asks for; or the resenting of unsolicited negative comments, even though they may be accurate. Also, one's own wrath dealt out to one's own relative is all right, but similar remarks by a stranger are not acceptable. See *reversal*.

CUNNILINGUS—oral contact with female genitals.

DNA—an abbreviation for a chemical substance that has an influence on inherited or genetic aspects of development.

DEFENSES—mental mechanisms which serve to protect people from inner impulses or anxiety.

DIDDLE—as used here, to manually fondle the genitals of a child by an adult.

EMPATHY—the capacity to put oneself into the position of another, to be able to feel what they feel.

EXISTENTIAL—from existentialism; the process or mode of being or living an authentic, "real" life and not merely going through the motions. Human responsibility for behavior and not reliance on the supernatural is implied.

FLAT—to express emotionally charged events without feeling tone; the absence of affect. See *toast and tea.*

FLIP—as used by Pam, an abrupt, short-lived injection of humor into sad or frustrating or angry moments. Flip is a distant cousin to optimism. Unrelated to glib.

FREUD, Sigmund—the founder of psychoanalysis, and the main pioneer from whom newer psychiatric theories have been derived.

GROUP THERAPY—one form of psychotherapy, of which there are many sub-forms, where people are simultaneously treated in a group, usually seven to ten in number.

HALLUCINATION—an auditory or visual perception of an external sound or object, when no such sound or object is present.

HOSTILE—feelings which do not have a specific object; free floating feelings of resentment or frustration without an identifiable motive. See *angry.*

I.U.D.—intrauterine device. A means of contraception by the placement of an inert object in the womb.

INDIVIDUAL THERAPY—psychotherapy in which there is a one to one relationship between the patient and the doctor.

INSIGHT—the coming into conscious awareness of the reason for abnormal or morbid feelings, often with a disappearance of the abnormal feelings after gaining the insight. Enlightenment.

JEWISH MOTHER—people, not confined to Jews and not confined to mothers, who "baby" their children, spouses, or parents to the point of being a gigantic pain in the rectum. See *mothering.*

JUNGIAN—reference is to psychological theories derived from the work of Carl Jung, which is heavily weighted with mystical and spiritual components.

LABEL (to LAY that on me)—to transfer one's own problems (hang-ups and guilty feelings) on to someone else.

Usually done unknowingly and usually to people who are meaningful to each other.

MOTHERING—excessive, overindulgent concern; does not occur only between a mother and child. See *Jewish mother.*

NEUROTIC (NEUROSIS)—an emotional disorder where one continues to be able to function despite emotional conflicts; reality boundries remain intact.

OEDIPUS THING (ref. OEDIPUS COMPLEX)—a normal phase in the sexual development of children, during which time the child experiences positive sexual feelings for the parent of the opposite sex.

PASSIVE-AGGRESSIVE—a personality disturbance where one is indirectly aggressive or hostile, as for example, in habitual lateness.

PATHOLOGY (ref. PSYCHOPATHOLOGY)—abnormal psychological development; the presence of emotional abnormality.

P.E. COMPLEX (PENIS ENVY)—a Freudian concept of jealousy in women for not having a penis; symbolically represented in women by "masculine" striving or overcompetitiveness.

PHENOMENOLOGY—to examine and evaluate events or phenomena. To appraise events objectively.

PROJECT (PROJECTION)—a mental mechanism where one attributes to others unliked aspects of one's own self. See *defenses.*

REAL—a person who is sensitive, receptive, and expressive of honest feelings; who is genuine and has substance and depth.

REVERSAL—to say one thing and to mean something else which is not stated with words; i.e., no, you don't have to close the window (said out loud), but I'm cold and I really want it closed (not spoken, but revealed nonverbally by body messages, i.e. shivering). A word used by Pam, which is really the *double-bind*.

SCHIZO LADIES (ref. SCHIZOPHRENIA)—a serious emotional illness where contact with reality is lost.

SYNANON—a group, not unlike Alcoholics Anonymous, that deals with people who voluntarily join to "cure" a drug problem.

THERE—that "place" or point of time in therapy which is experienced as quite painful, or meaningful, or difficult. Less often "there" may be a pleasurable revelation.

TOAST AND TEA—to speak or relate painful past events casually and without apparent feeling. See *flat*.

UNCONSCIOUS—that part of the mind where activities are carried on without one's direct awareness; the presence of the unconscious being known by inference via dreams, slips of the tongue, and so forth.

VASECTOMY—an operation which sterilizes a man, by cutting sperm-carrying tubes. There is no organic after-effect upon his ability to perform sexually.

VIBES—an abbreviation for vibrations or feelings received from others; a sensing of good or bad vibes (feelings) from others. Vibes can also arise from within and be directed toward others.

ZEN—dealing, as used here, with mystical or spiritual or nonlogical concerns.

616.8914
B512

85945